Katrina ... -ch!
I ...

Thank you for your attention!

Loud Whispers of Silent Souls

Poems

Published by Ibhubesi Books
P.O. Box 279004
Miramar, FL 33027-9004

Cover Illustration: Jason Cowell
Cover Design: C. L. Brown
Author Photo: Jason Cowell

Library of Congress Control Number: 2015905905

FIRST EDITION

ISBN: 0-9962013-0-0
ISBN-13: 978-0-9962013-0-8

Ibhubesi the Great

Loud Whispers of Silent Souls

Poems

C. L. BROWN

Contents

Whispers of **Broken Hearts**

Dedication

I dedicate this book to my beautiful Mother, Hyacinth Brown, who is now sleeping beautifully in peace. After my mother's passing I found a letter that she wrote. It was sort of a goodbye letter she had written a while back, perhaps during the time of her first battle with Breast Cancer. There was one line in that letter that ruptured something deep inside of me. My mother wrote that she wished she had done something great that her children would be proud of her. Even now as I recall those words I can feel the tears welling up inside my eyes. My mother was the type of mother that would give everything for her family. She sacrificed without a second thought if she knew that her family would be better for it. My mother loved me with a love I will never fully understand. During her first battle with Breast Cancer I recall sitting next to her in the hospital room the day after she was diagnosed. I was deeply sadden, but I was trying my best not to let her see that. I wanted to be strong for her. My mother looked up at me and said "I don't want you to fret." I thought to myself she is the one with the terminal illness, yet she was more concerned about me than herself. That is the love I knew. That is the love I know.

In 2005, for my 26th birthday, my mother started to write me a note. It simply said, "Prince from mom. Love Ya! Suppose one morning I never wake up. Do y" … That was it. I'm not sure why she stopped writing, perhaps she became distracted, but March 6th 2014 would be the morning she wrote about; the morning she didn't wake up. I found that note among some of her belongings after she passed.

I would not be the man I am today had it not been for my mother. She never one day gave me reason to doubt her immeasurable love for me. So this book I dedicate to you mom. I am so very proud of you and so very proud to call you mother for the remainder of my time. Yes, I do know that you love me. I love you too, forever!

Acknowledgements

Without the presence of some very special people in my life this book would not have come together. My father Earl, Grandmother Maud, brothers and sisters: Patricia, Michelle, Pamela, Perry, Donovan and Dwight. My dear friends: Chris, Keisha, Duane, Leon, Roan, Nicola, Debbie and Nicole. My cups of water: Tanya Donigan thank you for being as amazing as you are. Jason Cowell you are an example that I pay very close attention to. Thank you for all that you've done. Pablo Rivas you are the match that ignited the fuel… One conversation and I will never forget. Joy Sewell-Buchanan thank you for keeping me on track. Lesley-Ann Wright thank you for believing in me. Angelica Rosario, your name says it all. You are an Angel. Fallon Jallali there was a time when I didn't see, but through God's eyes you saw. You are amazing and I thank you. Melanie Alden your encouragement and support never lacks, thank you! To everyone else who has supported and encouraged me along this journey I am eternally grateful to you all. From the core of my Soul I thank you all.

Foreword

I was in an abusive situation for a few years and suffered silently for the most part. Through therapy you learn that most victims protect their abusers while in these situations. Most experience shock, confusion, betrayal, helplessness, hopelessness and an overwhelming sense of being alone. That was my ultimate struggle. No one would ever understand or so I thought, until I read *Hush Now Baby Girl.* A few years into our friendship, I decided to share my past abusive experience with Cliff, as I so affectionately call him. It must have been a four hour conversation. No more than forty five minutes after hanging up the phone did I receive an email entitled *'Hush Now Baby Girl'.* I was in awe. His ability to relate and speak directly to me on such a personal and sensitive issue was absolutely mind blowing.

Upon initial meeting, unless he's dancing, Cliff may appear shy and a bit reserved. Once relaxed, he's a great conversationalist and a jokester. He also loves to eat or as he puts it, has a "great appreciation for the advancement of the culinary arts". He loves his family and since his mom's passing last year has made every effort to communicate that even more so with them. ***Loud Whispers of Silent Souls*** is dedicated to his mom whom I know is smiling with such pride that only a parent can possess. Hyacinth, the precious flower I've only known through his words, is the gentle, kind and soft spoken mother whose scent is that of a delicate lily. Her smile is not the blinding noon time sun, but rather the perfectly setting sun cradling the horizon. Cliff, her Prince as she nicknamed him at birth, is the kind hearted soul she raised him to be and the gentleman she would be proud of. His love and adoration for her are poured out in *Hyacinth's Flower* in the chapter *Whispers of My Mother.*

Cliff is exceedingly hard-working and will stop at nothing to achieve his dreams. This dream of writing a book of poetry has been one for a few years now and his drive and determination has never waned regardless of how difficult or impossible this dream may have seemed at times. He would faithfully steal away to a quite spot, whether it's close to a pond or just some trees providing shelter and write his heart out. When he puts pen to paper he becomes superhuman because it is just so unexpected. The strength and power behind and within his words are magnetic, inspiring, fulfilling, revealing, soul bearing, erotic, sensual, and relatable yet out of this world. There are pieces within this book that will have you feeling completely exposed because of their relatability, but there are also those that will leave behind a desire for a feeling you've never experienced.

Cliff can draw inspiration from air… literally. I remember the first time I found out about his passion for writing. He was in Jamaica for a funeral almost 9 years ago. While in Jamaica he messaged me saying how inspired he was by the lush outdoors on the island. He spoke as though he had just completed the most intimate of conversations with nature. The interaction that he described, the picture that he painted through his words, was one of the most vivid I had ever imagined; it was at that moment that I recognized the talent that my 'IT friend' possessed. It was also at that very moment that I learned about his respect towards nature and his yearning for all things spiritual. In the chapter *Whispers of Inner Meditation*, the pieces *Supplications of a Misplaced Soul* and *Coming Forth by Day* captures the hunger that he has for learning and living a life that is grounded in spirituality.

He is a dreamer and a hopeless romantic (even though he doesn't yet recognize this) and appears to be a devouring lover, but you will know once you've completed reading chapters *Whispers of Love*, *Whispers of Passion* and *Whispers of Broken Hearts*. He will take you on a journey of friendship *(Unquenched)* to new love *(New Love)*, through a love just for two *(They Will Never Understand)*, fill you with confidence that glows *(Ode to Woman)* and then tops it with *(Naked Night's Silence)* a passionate lip-biting, intense back-scraping and sensual love making session. And then… *Black Sunday*. The most transparent and vulnerable piece within these three chapters of love and love lost, as it highlights Cliff's very raw emotion of devastation when his fiancée unexpectedly called off their wedding just a few months before the date. Though we've had many conversations about that failed relationship, none of them quite captured his real feelings towards the situation like this poem has. It is one of my absolute favorites.

It was truly an honor to have been given a front row seat on this journey with Cliff. ***Loud Whispers of Silent Souls*** is the book you simply must have in your library. Its diversity will speak to and about you. It will speak to and about someone that you know. Cliff is a genuine and authentic writer whose art is refreshing to witness. This is just the beginning for Cliff and I expect a lot more to come; as will you, once you have taken this incredible journey with him.

Tanya Donigan
March 10, 2015
Pembroke Pines, Florida

Whispers of Love

Love is the art of servants. If you are not willing to serve you are not ready to love.

Conversation

She said, "write me a poem"
I said you are my poem,
already written,
fused with every thought that traverses my mind
She said, "read it to me"
I said I do that every time I touch you
I said this pen bled my thoughts and every word was your name
She smiled
I said I open my lips
I kiss your lips
I taste your soul
Now I crave you like never before
I traced the contour of her face with my fingers
She said, "why do you do that?"
I said I love painting your portrait inside my soul
I said a thousand places I have journeyed,
but I'm home only when I'm with you
I said, when I look into your eyes I can't remember my lines
I try and try to remember past times but… I can't see past you
She said, "tell me more"
I said your eyes are the doorway to my peace
I said your mouth is an instrument serenading my soul;
playing for me the sweetest melodies,
enchanting me as your lips move with the spirit of the spoken word
I lose myself with every beautiful word that breaks your lips
I said when you caress my face you take all my strength,
but I'm OK with that
I said I'm staying
She said "Where?"
I said with you, I'm staying
She said "Why?"
I said because outside of you lie only death and I so badly want to live

She breathed in deeply
She said "When did you write this poem?"
I said the day you were born
Her eyes grew soft and her smile faded into the penumbra
She looked deep into my eyes and said "I do not understand"
I said, when your soul was created
  a void inside me was instantly filled
I said till now I have waited all of my life seeking you,
  waiting to see you,
    wanting to touch you,
      needing to hold you
        and now here you are in my arms, my beautiful poem
Her eyes flooded, then I kissed them
Her smile resurfaced and I smiled back
She said, "I really love this poem"
I said, I've always loved you

Stay

When the morning comes and you've gone away
My arms hug your memory
My lips kiss the illusion
My eyes see the smile you gave after amazing love
And when the morning comes,
    when you've gone away
My heart still quakes
My skin is still stained with your fingers' prints
My soul still smells like you
    and I'd have it no other way
You should know my today I will trade for yesterday
    hoping tomorrow will be as today's eve
But my tomorrow can be my yesterday
    if today you'll just stay

Dancing Shadows

The candle stood in solitude flickering its flame,
casting its silhouette against my soul
The residue of rain drops romping on tin roof,
beating against inquisitive leaves in their falling
Flashes of lightening invading our privacy,
erasing images painted of the lone flame
Pressed firmly against each other
Feet intertwined
as though there was room for just one on the king-sized bed
The softness of her fingers gliding over my face
Repeating herself trying to convey a message I hadn't yet understood
Time and space has never felt so good
Lost in the window of her soul
She smiled
I noticed, and made my inquiry
"Oh it's nothing" she said
But I held strong to persistence
"I've thought many times what life would be like without you" she said
I interrupted, "like a bee without honey?"
She smiled again, "Yes, like a bee without honey"
"Like a heart without a beat?"
She chuckled, "You're so crazy, but yes! Like a heart without a beat"
"How about like a tree without her leaves,
the morning without the sun's rise,
like the night sky without a single star or
like the ocean without the sound of her waves?"
She got quiet thinking on all those things
Breaking silence she spoke, "Yes my love, like all those things"
She took a deep breath in preparation for the words
that had broken free from her heart seeking a place on her lips
I interrupted, "then now I know I am not alone"
She smiled and I was taken away

There isn't any such thing as unconditional love. If there is such a thing as unconditional love that implies there is also conditional love. But true love can't be conditional can it? You can't chose when to and when not to love based on something that is favorable to you. That is not love. Love is simply that, LOVE. It doesn't need any adjectives such as "unconditional" added to it. So just love, simply LOVE.

Intrusion

As the rising of sleeping tides,
    when the prying moon peruses oceans' secrets
Her voice like an adept cello
    rehearsed the secret tune inside his doleful soul
Their juvenile love spoke conspicuously of eager hearts
    when she eclipsed his fears as when the sun
    and the moon meet in one place
Her sightless fingers passed over his pitted skin reading unspoken
    poetry as time aged
Time aged in the patience of her piercing eyes invading his
    timorous silence
She is freedom's wings uprooting his anchored thoughts
She is freedom's wings, uprooting his anchored thoughts

Suppose

Suppose tonight just before you say how angry you are I place my
fingers on your lips and hushed your inner troubles?
Suppose on a simple Tuesday morning just as the sun breaks the
eastern horizon I kissed your forehead waking you for the
breakfast I placed on the night stand next to you?
Suppose I wrote the words of our song on the bathroom mirror for
you to sing while brushing your teeth in the morning?
Suppose I hold you in my arms and watch you fall asleep
to see you when you are most still?
Suppose when my heart hurts I replay the messages you left on my
phone just because your voice heals me?
Suppose when I say I love you the words are actually
echoing from my soul?
Suppose your touch comforts me like nothing else can?
Suppose I anxiously await the passing of the night just
to see you next to me at dawn?
Suppose I still the sun at its setting until you've had your fill?
Suppose I dance with you through the rain while my love quiets your
fear of the lightening?
Suppose I send a songbird to sing to you my love when I'm missing you
and distance will not have me to touch you?
Suppose I vowed never to leave you one step behind?
Suppose I love you in and out of time?
Suppose when you read these words I am standing in front of you?
Suppose it's the first time I'm seeing you?
Suppose right now I'm actually missing you?
Suppose this poem is actually about you?
Just, suppose

Hidden Hearts and Open Secrets

You penetrate my truth with tender eyes;
searching my desolate soul
revealing secrets I've hidden from aged love
And like sacred waters making anew the fallen,
unspoken words from your quieted lips restored my brokenness
I now live only in the residue of your love;
a captive of time's patience and
the ocean's waters taunt my falling at the knees;
tears streaming down my face
like thirsty rivers rushing to open seas

I crave you
I crave the feel of the wind leaving your alluring skin
I desire to read your story beautifully written within
I crave the sight of your smile
and my soul anticipates the drink of a love I have not known
When I close my eyes taking you in stars fall from grace,
but I will never take my eyes off of you

Do you know how often I think of you?
How often I compose loose thoughts submerged in unanswered questions,
but my soul wants to love you forever
and to that stands no question
In the quiet of my mind I still time
pouring all of you into all of me
Rewinding time I find you at our inception
when our passion gave us reason though reason stood contrary
Do you know how much I miss you?

My sweetest pleasure is knowing time will never have you
and relentlessly I'll chase you until time grows feeble
Our love is unspoken poetry

And the taste of your lips between mine without account of time
when our souls needed reassurance still reassures me;
when your arms embraced me intimately
and your eyes grew soft
when my heart bled hallowed secrets bearing your name

I'd rather have you
I'd rather your fingers against my skin
I'd rather the sight of your hair undulating in the wind
than to be bathed in secrets the heavens have not spoken

Well I remember the night the star-lit skies stole your eyes
We made love in the secret of a thought still unspoken
We conversed without words
and our bodies sung Moonlight Sonata

I remember your smile
and it is still the prettiest thing
Do you know how often I exhaust time
watching you sit still in the quiet of my mind?
Do you know how much, I love you?

Any woman can open her mouth and speak to a man. It takes a special woman to open her mouth and strengthen a man.

Unquenched

When she is your everything she will occupy everything about you
Her smile in your mind you will see more times
    than seconds in the longest day
When she cries you'll pray her pain away
When prayers will have no part of it you will hold her
    until her soul finds peace
Try as you may you will never stop till you've touched every
    inch of her soul

She's known fear, that old snare that despises free souls,
    but I can hear the silent song her caged heart now sings
She cries for freedom
She's my sweetest temptation
I'll never have enough
I'll never give fear a chance to conceal the words I composed
    when I thought to satisfy her soul
I've stolen God's time because for her I'll give patience
    every reason to be
I'm acquainted with her, though my name she does not know
But when my thoughts get chaotic she is the source of my peace

Your Long Awaited

Smiles break sad lips
Happy eyes hide unhappy tears
Hearts melt in it all,
    when love suddenly comes

I kissed her forehead and her heart felt OK
Picture perfect this perfectly depicted moment
I held her and our lips became intimate

Stars gazed and the moon lit her face
    just enough for me to see just how beautiful she really is
The wind took her sent to my soul and that's all I needed

Yesterday is gone
Today is neglected,
    but at no fault of my own
Because the heart would rather have her in yesterday than live today in void

She wonders why I chose her,
    but when she came there was no longer a choice
Forsake your fears thinking on yester-years
Today is here and so is the best we'll ever have
Well hello darling...
It is good to finally meet you
I am your long awaited

Soul's Mate

Tell me of the woman who touches me with purpose
    and I will know my soul's mate
Ask me about Heaven
    and I will tell you about her eyes
Let her sleep quietly in my arms
    that I may see her soul when she's most still
Try if you will to separate her from my love
Rather try if you will to still the wind
    because your chances are greater
She speaks of me with a tongue only the heavens understand
She looks at me,
    but sees not flesh
Her essence is sweet poetry rolling off my tongue
I taste her then close my lips to savor the life she bequeathed me
So take the stars of the night because she is my light
She will ask and I will empty my soul that she may have life
Her love is mine
    and my love she'll have beyond the reaches of time
So tell me of the woman who touches me with purpose
    and speak well of my soul's mate

Never compete with someone's possessions. You are worth so much more.

Simple, but the Most Beautiful

Your eyes are a mirror to my soul
I smiled at my reflection,
    but it was you that I saw
I reached grabbing hold of my miracle,
    then you walked over
Never have I seen such grace in one's steps
Simple, but the most beautiful

Like stars slow dancing in the moon's light when love sung her heart out,
    we danced in the quietude of my love
        when I drew forth your celestial essence
Your silence is divine remedy
    when quietly my soul rests in your love

There is a song that nuzzles my soul
The melody, angelic to say the least
The song is yours
The song is you
The only song I will ever dance to
You are simple, but you are the most beautiful

Black Violin

Play my sweet music to your heart's content
I was the wind, snared;
encaged by misunderstanding
though I sang beautifully for his freedom
My song was taken until you came,
playing your black violin

You are love nestled in the arms of patience,
testing my patience until I came forth as pure gold
I waited for you
I waited beyond the confines of time
I waited for you
Praying that before death I'd be awaken
and then you came,
playing your black violin

I've searched for my voice throughout time,
at times losing my mind until I heard you
and found me
I will listen
Share with me the splendor of your essence
I will listen
I will keep you until the end of everything
because you soothe my pain
each time you play that black violin

You are God's wisdom and patience personified,
perfectly crafted into my soul's deepest desire
Your voice comes to me and my troubles are exorcised
And how gracefully your fingers move over my broken soul
like the master musician plucking violin cords;
restoring the pieces those before you selfishly stole

Now my heart knows light
Now my soul is awakened
by the notes bellowing
from your black violin

My freed thoughts are now your slave
Song birds are quieted as notes you played
sitting there quietly in the comfort of my shade
So strum my soul with songs of love
Tune me from within with songs my love
Allow my tempo to rise and to fall on the notes flowing
from your black violin

Free spirits abide in the sacred thoughts of the silent wind
Your spirit abides in my thoughts hidden deeply within
Many played for me before you came,
but I waited still
I waited
I am yours still
I think always of you, even in the depth of night
when the moon reveals the sun's hiding
At times finding myself standing beneath the moon-lit sky
dancing to the notes you played from your black violin

My soul trusts your song
Your tone invades my being
I dare not rush perfection because you're perfected with time
And perfect love casts all my sins while I sit still,
listening to you playing your black violin

In my mind I frequent heaven
and when the eye sees,
all I ever see is you
Conversant soul,
your sweet pleasures I have never known,

but our lips touched
and somehow I know now I knew you before this;
perhaps in another life,
maybe in another song

But if tomorrow should be and I am not,
know that I carry you within the sacred abode of my silent wind
And if I awake to learn I have not a single thing,
I know for certain,
deep within I'll still have the notes you played
from your beautiful black violin

Her

Her velvet skin is the like of untainted chocolate
Her smile lights the sun
Her eyes tell your story
Her touch says you're never alone
Her fingers remind you of home
Her scent takes your mind away
Her love is your soul's remedy,
    why would you stray?
Her embrace is fire to the troubles written on your mind
Her kiss is your provision
Her hips are your prison
Watch how she moves with precision
Close your eyes
She is your vision

A good woman is a priceless find. Never insult her by putting a price on her. A woman is a recipient. Put good things in her and she will be a blessing all your days. Put bad things and you cause even your own soul to decay.

Letter to My Unknown

I've seen your smile though I've never seen your face
I've laughed at your jokes yet we've never spoken
I've kissed away your tears but we've never touched
You are so beautiful,
    just the way you are

You were without understanding when first we met
I saw it in your eyes
Felt it in your breath
You felt my soul then everything felt right
Then you looked at me
Then you smiled so bright
I said just enough to quiet your fears though I spoke not a single word
I prayed, I asked God to let you watch over my rest
    while I escape this tangible existence
I told Him, "Give my angel to another"
Because you're all that I need when reality fades
    and the soul searches for the meaning life

I whisper "good morning" to you my every waking day
I kiss your eyes each night while you sleep the night away
We've walked beneath the stars,
    kissed beneath the moon,
        and woke to the rising sun,
            but it never gets old,
                not with you
I carry you with me all the time
But please don't hesitate to stop by sometime

Comforter

She invokes smiles amidst selfish tears
    whispering sweet lullabies of love when I need her most
I need her most when selfish tears sentence my thoughts
    where happy souls venture not
She is mountains' tears when I lie empty beneath her provisions,
    dried up,
        awaiting my fill

Silhouette of an Unspoken Thought

She came to me bearing bad dreams and fears
    then my mind spoke to the keepers of everything
        and our souls connected in that way they always do

Thoughts of our tumultuous past gave reason not to answer the call
    but my heart missed her
        and my hands itched
            to touch the body my lips longed to kiss

There were no smiles
No laughter
But I held her
    then she wept on my shoulder;
Mascara and eyeliner smearing my white shirt
    as cold tears seeped into my skin

The room was silent save the soundtrack of our past love
    playing in that present space
My mind drifted from the dry place my soul spent latter days
    to the sea of love
        where I met love
            in the eyes of the woman I'm now letting go

She said, "You don't feel like home anymore"
Her arms felt strange
My eyes invaded her soul and nothing felt out of place
Before it was over, "I love you" she whispered;
    her head finding comfort on my shoulder
Then the sun came through the clouds that hovered my soul
    and she flew back to the place I am no longer welcome
        after whispering,
            "You feel like home again"

Don't misuse your brain by trying to love with it.

Don't misuse your heart by trying to think with it.

Of the Angels

That moment when she becomes the river
        taking your soul to the great deep
She's your sea of reception
Go under, she's your air
Stay under, she's your covering
Kiss when bubbles send Love's truth rising to surface's face
Tell her she's your everything
Be all that she ever needs
She is blossoms of cherry
        embellishing the dull sadness of your unattended ground
Flavors of heaven overwhelms your soul
        when tastes of her lips reveal the hidden essence of God's
                best kept secret
I've laid till the moon sung to the closing of her eyes
I have seen my angel asleep
She came and I spoke
She touched me and
        poems flowed like mountains' waters when desolate valleys
                cry for life
I will tell you about her body
How she pulls strength from me
        when her fingers search my soul
To lie against her nakedness
To see her soul unclothed
She is the glory of God and my soul's most loved
I will tell you of the beauty hidden behind her eyes
Search the heavens
Search the earth
Exhaust time
        and speak of the beauty which has no equal
She is blossoms of cherry
        embellishing the dull sadness of my unattended ground

She

She watched the sea washing the sun and I saw the moon rise in her bosom
She looked at me and sung then I submitted to wisdom
My death slept in her life and memories conveyed time I haven't yet seen
She is my vision
She is an ocean of stars in my lightless prison
She is my love song
The inspiration for this poem

Through birds she serenade me
In trees she dances for me
Through the wind she touches me
In my dreams she comes to me
She is an ocean of stars in my lifeless void
She asked of me nothing
In return I gave her everything

How Much?

Can you love her still when jealously makes her seem a little crazy?
When she lies a little longer in bed
    because the soothing rain makes her lazy?
And if she cries when you turn away
    do you love her enough to change your mind,
        to stay?
Do you love the kisses she give when you occupy her time?
Do you tell her often "baby all you have I wish to be mine"?
If she can't carry on do you love her enough to finish her story?
When her heart's weary do you give her reasons not to worry?
Do you squeeze when you hug as though her skin you'll never read again?
Will you carry her in your soul till your very end?

Love is a responsibility for which we will be held accountable once we decide to tell someone that we love them; even if that person does not hold us accountable, Life will.

Orchid

Orchid, wind dancer
Colors radiating beauty without apology, stealing the eyes of love
Graceful spirit moved by the hand unseen;
        shifting in time,
        between time,
        defying time
Your beauty is unrivaled
Age you do not know
Silent bellows rose from your deep infusing my openness

Listen to the mighty voice of oceans' waves dancing in your wind
You soothe my mind
A droplet of tear caress your face intimately, enticing my envy
Permit me and I will drink of your provisions
Rise with the morning's light
Share your life with those wise enough to toss mundane pleasures
Extended hands clasp embracing love in her purest form
Shed your tears and old burdens are no more

The graceful flight of silent leaves racing to kiss silent ground
        and here you are hands in mine
Dare you embrace this time in time
Dare you smile
Orchid, wind dancer
Colors radiating beauty without apology, stealing the eyes of love
There you sat in the splendor of your beauty
When a thousand stars faded in your smile
A thousand lives spared

Heal these broken thoughts with only your touch
Heal this broken soul with your unspoken essence
Dance evermore to this song looping within,

the song of the wind, composed by the soul unknown
You enthrall me
You enthrall me graceful spirit dancing in the wind;
shifting in time,
between time,
defying time
Beauty unrivaled, age you do not know

Break the rainbow
Separate her colors one from the other
Tell me, is this possible?
Break this bond, this love, this imperfect love perfectly given
Tell me, is this possible?
Tainted is all that I touch, but in the palms of my soul you remain perfect
You are my Orchid silently serenading my soul with every sway
when your wind blows my way
My Orchid, dancing in the wind to everything my heart desires to say
My Orchid, gracefully dancing in my soul
My Orchid, dancing inside my love

A Song in Love's Arms

I'm still in love with you
With everything about you
With your eyes, how they pierce me
With your touch, how you possess me
With your lips, how they heal me
With your visits into my quiet space

With the feel I get when our souls connect making deep love
With laying against your nakedness trying to catch our breaths
    after we're both satisfied of Love's making
With my fingers caressing your back,
    squeezing your skin
With my hands cuffing your butt cheeks each time we meet
    and I pull you in
With you sleeping on top of me
With our days spent lost inside every song played

I still dream, even while awake
Hoping someday my hands, my apology you will take
I'm still dreaming not ready to be awake,
    not yet
        and don't ask me to because I won't be
Not purposely
Not yet

Lilly of the Rain

There stood I before a blooming rose mind set on the lone Lilly
  dancing in her rain
But to dine with love one must accept the counsel of the heart
Thus I lost sight of everything in the here and now
There is no here
There is no now
Because I am there with my Lilly dancing in her rain

What is it to walk willingly into darkness seeing there is no light?
Faith? Perhaps…
Folly? I beg to differ
What difficulty must I face pursuing you in this sea of souls?
Madness is watching you dance with another when our song plays
I've had my share of madness
I want nothing more than to dance with my Lilly soaked in her rain

The heart grows weak each time my eyes perceive you
Today I feast on a memory because I still crave you
Perhaps greed has gotten the best of me,
  but who am I to deny myself her pleasures?
At least my tongue is pleased, reminding my soul what
  awaits him in the hereafter

You are the delight of my eyes
I want to taste you in every imaginable way
I want to see you in every imaginable way
I want to kiss you wiping those tears away
I want to touch you driving those fears away
Because fear has no place, not here, not with me
Not when I desire only you, in every imaginable way
To dance with you in your pouring rain

Love is the foundation of life. Don't believe that? Completely remove love from your existence and see what you have left. When we are broken time has proven again and again that the best remedy is Love. When we are most joyous just look around; I bet somewhere close by you will find Love orchestrating the entire thing. So when they ask "what's love got to do with it?" Look them square in the eyes and say, "everything!"

Love Letter to My Love

My love
Love of my life
My breath
The repetitious beats of my heart
Why has your countenance fallen?
Why are your cheeks saturated with tears?
Your beautiful cheeks that my lips long so much to kiss

My air, why is your heart weary?
Your heart no longer dances to the song in mine
Why does your heart skip vital beats as an old man gasping for air
after a day's journey?

My love, your eyes
Where is the luster that once took residence in your eyes?
How many are the days that your beautiful eyes have comforted me
Where now must I turn when my burdens are too much to bear?
I can no longer free myself from them with one stare into your eyes
Those beautiful eyes, why have they hid themselves from me?

My love
My life
My heart
My strength
Take my hands
Take my hands that I may take you back to that place
Do you remember that place?
Does your heart see?
That place… That magical place where tears are forbidden to flow
That place whose very hands created love
That place where LOVE, is

Think of the gardens my sweetheart
Those ageless gardens where flowers of a thousand sort beguile
curious eyes
Think of the butterflies that found rest in your hair each time they
beheld your beauty
Think of that place

Do you remember now?
Has it come back to you?
Do you remember that fruit?
It was your favorite
Do you remember how when you bit into it its juices overwhelmed
your mouth and flowed like a relentless stream over your lips?
I must take you back to that place
That place where LOVE, is
So my love
My air
My heart
My life
You must now take my hands
You must now take my hands for I must take you to that place where
your countenance rose like the mountains there in
That place where I kissed you in the company of the wind
That place where my love was the fortress no other could enter in

My love
My heart
My darling
My breath
At last!
At last your tear-free cheeks have once again greeted my lips
At last my lips have once again burst into smiles
At last I can lay my burdens down for the luster in your eyes
have returned to me
At last my heart rejoices in me, for it can now hear your heart

dancing to its song

My love
My, LOVE!
My life
My breath
My joy
My strength
My air
It does me well to see you again, My LOVE!

For Love

For love I will wait my life's time and if by chance she doesn't come I will walk the brink of death in my immortal days until her soul and mine knows no separation

For love I will give her eyes a million reasons not to cry and if by chance she finds a million and one, I will cry with her until we cleanse her soul

For love I will watch her sleep when the sun finds his rest and if by chance she should awake before the moon goes away I will hold her till her eyes grew too weary to stare

For love I will call her name and if by chance another answers I will seek her soul because it has no equal in this life or the next

For love I will write songs, poems, and quotes to inspire her and if by chance her soul is still not acquainted with peace, I will sit with her until we find her healing

For love I will pray for her and if by chance her burdens do not grow lighter I will ask God to permit me to share her load

For love I will do all these things and if by chance she is still wondering I will read this to her every night until she truly understands that she alone completes me

I Love You Forever

When the riches of time I have stolen
    and the unnoticed lines in my skin become bold wrinkles
When the summer's heat dries the spring's rains
    and the winter's cold puts the heat to shame,
    always, you are my love

When your imperfections hide your confidence
    and your tears prevent you from seeing the smile on my face
    when my heart whispers to you softly,
    my love will never fade
My love, will never fade

When you have nothing to give but a kiss
    and nothing to comfort me but a hug,
    I will swim the immense breadth of the oceans to receive this gift
So kiss me!
Kiss me my beautiful love, because I love you
I love you!
I love you!
I, love you!

If your heart is not at risk of being broken your love is not worth having.

Rambling

And then there's that moment when absolutely everything feels perfect
The truth is, it's really not,
        but you sneak some time away from the madness at hand
        and you think of her
You imagine that smile that seem to always compel you to smile
She's a darling and a sweetheart
When she touches you time suspends itself
        selflessly giving you enough of itself to take a piece of her soul
        so you'll never be too far from heaven
Then you thank God because you say only Him
And it seem troubles are afraid
        because they never come around when she's near
Passionate kisses,
        intimate hugs
        and eyes that penetrate the deepest parts of you
She sees you even when you try to hide from yourself
So you think of her
Then you ramble on about it and everyone wonders,
        but mystery at times is so lovely,
        though never enough to match her beauty

They Will Never Understand

They will never understand why it is I love you so much
They will never understand why I trust you with all of me;
  why every time we meet
  you thrill me from my head to my feet
They will never understand how it is you woo my soul
  and cause my heart to fall for everything about you
Your sweet embrace is my great escape
You hold me without hands, but I'm never more intimately held
You know well my vibration
You take me high and low singing with me the same beautiful song
Days away from you are the worst because I hunger for you
  and there is no substitute for the taste of heaven
They ask why I speak so much of you
I tell them my soul craves you and I simply can't have enough
Even now I am here with you,
  inside of you
  and you inside of me
  yet still I'm missing you
You've shown me things and taken me places I'd never imagine
You speak and I listen well learning the teachings of love
To heaven you bridge me
  allowing me to see the God in me
I've had thoughts wondering why you took so long to come
Wondering why you took so long to show me who you are
But I understand now that perfection has a place of birth
  and a time of fruition,
    but they will never understand

Still

You are my reflection in truth's mirror
Around you darkness loses its terror
When I'm broken you put together every splinter
I've had my feast of bitterness,
        but when I taste of your skin
        it is still the sweetest thing
Reach deep within
Draw from my soul the passion I've stored many years
Draw near that I may touch your face and kiss those tears
I know I gave them reasons to flow,
        but I promise it won't always be that way
Yesterday I thought about the emptiness of tomorrow,
        but today you're still mine
Still my sun shines
I still write beautiful poetry
        and you still inspire me
Your you and my me is still a beautiful concoction of random sweet
        with a tiny bit sour,
                but that's OK
                        because the us that we are is still my favorite flower

---

When the heart is not content it signifies a deep imbalance within the soul. Whatever you do find it and fix it.

Invaded Space

I write simple words because you're simply beautiful
I kiss you slowly because my lips love reading your story
I tell them about you when they ask of things that make me happy
I listen to the radio, but the songs you love I play in my soul
I sit in the office, but my mind always go back to you
I can't wait for Saturday morning so we can lie in wrinkled sheets
    listening to the wind ruffling leaves outside my window
I love the residue of the clouds because we met once in the rain
I love when the lights go out allowing me to see you without eyes
I love the lines that form next to your eyes when your lips are happy
I'm just saying, I love you,
    the simple yet intricately beautiful you

Ode to Woman

She is diverse flowers of love rooted in sacred life
She is colors of earth, and the ocean's water hides in her eyes
Her words convey beautiful secrets the heavens whisper
Her eyes give birth to stars manifesting secret wishes
On her face the moon rose,
    pining for a glance at what time has no mastery of
Skin as soft as cotton reflecting light,
    casting shadows,
    whispering sonnets of love
Converse with her soul and know the genesis of life
Give attention to her discretion
    and taste of flavors foreign to those unfamiliar
Her love speaks truth though its interpretation's sung by men blinded with
    misguided motives
She is more than flesh,
    defying beauty's definition hidden in pretty faces and
    perfection's a myth if within her you can't find it
Be taken when her cord is playing because she plays for you
Orchestras recite her sonata
Brushes tell her story to canvas and bids outside of love are not heard
She is poetry intimate with soul-soothing music in the quiet of
    the summer day's twilight
Lips red as aged grapes take bits of my sanity as I take sips of her passion
Within she carries the sacred essence of life
    giving birth to impossibilities in her rightful time
In her arms fear is that which love casts forth
    and her mind's womb bear fruit desired
    of the brave souls who dare enter
Do not misread the melting of her eyes
    for it is a sign she has set things behind
She is a woman, but who can find her?

Just Enough

My shoulders aren't much,
but there is room enough for your face when your heart hurts most
My hands aren't much,
but they will always remind you you're not alone
My eyes aren't much,
but they will see the only beauty the heavens envy
My lips aren't much,
but they will never have your lips to be lonely
My tongue isn't much,
but when the heart flows over, it will share his secrets
and you will know like you there is no other
My feet aren't much,
but they will walk with you wherever it is your soul desires to go
and when your feet have had enough they will carry you
until we've found your purpose
My ears aren't much,
but empty your soul and not one word will go unheard
My mind isn't much,
but it thinks of you all the time
My heart isn't much,
but it will love just you until time grows old;
when nothing remains but the memory of the Love time couldn't lay to rest

---

Love is a simple truth. We were created in love of Love. You can be taught to hate because hatred is not inherent, but no one can teach you how to love because the very essence of your existence is love. To hate is to delude your true self yet even the hateful can be brought back to their true self, bearing the conviction of love.

New Love

She is my lovely
The star my Soul makes wishes upon
The lady who takes free time away from my mind
The one I said would come and draw from me sacred poems
I lie at night against the bareness of her skin
I touch her face painting dreams
I taste her essence in intimate kisses given
Ahhh my soul
My delighted soul

Dreams of Her Reality

Grounded beauty of shimmering colors
My dove, freely roaming through dreams of my awakened state
I see you like no one else
I see you and no one else
You were perfect and I stood looking
I promise I'll never turn away
Grounded beauty of shimmering colors
My dove, freely roaming through dreams of my awakened state
Love finding her place
Love finding her pace
Brokenness you won't find in my arms of strength and grace
I will carry you to a better place
Where physicality has no bearing
I will tell you how beautiful you are until you shed burdens becoming mine
Grounded beauty of shimmering colors
My dove, freely roaming through dreams of my awakened state
The voice of the unseen perfectly heard
Perfectly mended her grief
Then her beauty became as the Lilly when spring whispers at her leaves
Untainted among darkness
I see you through the darkness
Your colors shimmer in the darkness
As freely you roam through dreams of my awakened state

Irrational

When was it that Love became something to rationalize?
Are hearts not to be free?
To love like the wind blows,
    without consideration,
    without intent;
    just to be engulfed in raw passion
    and the divinely pure nature of candid feelings
    feeling all emotions
    when lovers' souls hide inside flesh
    that they may spend time sharing space
    lost inside each other learning everything about themselves

But the mind thinks,
    rationalizing what cannot be rationalized,
    the language of hearts
    spoken by souls who met beyond time
    when love struck in one perfect material-free place as
    lightening and nevermore will be

I think of her and she comes to me

She reads my poetry and conjures my soul
    when I am away in the totality of myself,
    but I run to her
    and drink from her soul Love's sacred truth
    to be renewed again
    as I do each time I slip too far from my weakness found in her skin

I'm seeking answers
    through prayers imbued with questions
    when my mind goes to her,
    and the heart refuses to close the door

because my eyes get lost in the windows of her soul
seeing everything that snared me when her lips spoke "hello"
and the world vanished instantaneously;
then I saw the Love I was to love
and lost sight of everything that had no part of her

But the sun does not shine long enough before clouds come
and bits of truth come piercing through
but not nearly long enough that I may see the end of us;
so I rationalize my irrational thoughts
but crave still the woman who draws from me all things beautiful

Longing For

Many moons have come and gone
Many stars rose to the height of their glory
then fell from grace across the night sky
Many are the days that the sun broke the eastern horizon
declaring the wondrous works of the Most High
Many are the days I have held her quietly as the clouds cried
Many are the smiles,
the laughter,
the tears I have seen upon the face of my beloved
Many are the days that my hungry eyes fed upon her beauty,
yet still without my fill
Too many are the days she spoke to my soul
alleviating the things I care not for
Many are the nights I fervently pray
her journey home is met with immeasurable peace
She is my well beloved
She is, my well beloved

Limitlessly Bounded

But what if I paid no attention to time;
giving all my possessions for your eyes,
the way they see through me when love speaks on your behalf?
What if I need to love just you,
forever,
whatever forever may be?
And when death finally comes,
what if I gladly gave him my body
because it is my soul that you occupy?
Would you have me still where stars are our playground
and suns have no purpose?
Would you stand by me still if heaven is a myth but I vow to love you till
we find what dying souls hope for?
What if we could live again, in love again, through all the cycles of time?
Through the ups when you laugh uncontrollably;
through the downs when I kiss you repeatedly
until definitively you know that you have all of me?
What if I paid no attention to time?

What if without her voice,
without the sound of her laughter,
he dies slowly where death had no dominance?
What if through her delicate hands he saw her broken pieces?
What if he took from himself the remedy her heart really needed?
Would that satisfy her soul?
Would his unfailing love again make her whole?

And what if he gave up the sound of passing comets
and the sight of star-bathing moons
for a chance to chase her until time is no longer?
What if he reminds her of the very best of her that her lips
and his skin never part as their hands lock sealing forever?

Would she be the light upon his beautiful darkness?
Would she heal his broken soul through her divine lips?
Would she understand his caressing of her skin?
Would she stay forever, with just him?
He would fall from grace if only to be her king
But would she stay forever, with just him?
What if he paid no attention to time?

Slave

You make me
BELIEVE!
in Soul Mates
TRAPPED inside your skin
a PRISONER of LOVE
I have no PLACE
I have no TIME
Not outside of you
so I can't go
not away
not from YOU

You take me IN
you take EVERYTHING
My Moon snared in the Sun's darkness
I've subdued her LIGHT
in FEAR
Your tears water my dry ground
but there is no RAINBOW of HOPE
in your eyes
You Lie With ME
FREELY!
I AM your FOOL
You read my eyes
but can't see my LIES
hidden DEEPLY behind
Your heart has no room
Your mind is too busy to decipher the DANGER in my touch
But, I LOVE YOU
more than you'll ever know

MY embrace is your DEATH

Your SOUL I slowly eat
TRUTH has no freedom
NOT outside of PAIN
So I keep you
BOUND!
Your heart breaking SLOWLY
Confused and LONELY
in the cold room of my COMPANY

CONFUSED by my touch
when my WORDS dictate poison
You are
my SLAVE!

TIME warns me
SONGS compel me
My HEART gives me REASON
Reason to stay
My mind says go, go away
but this LOVE
I am her SLAVE
YOUR SLAVE!
I HAVE become ALL that I have written
All that I have SPOKEN
Your monster
Your Lover
Your Hero
You see BEAUTY in my CHAOS
My SELFISHNESS
My self-inflicted MADNESS
wanting HER
needing YOU
A slave to my perpetual confusion
TRAPPED in my WORLD
where LOVE rules

where YOU
are the most PRECIOUS
where you are my SLAVE
willingly!
Where TRUTH has no FREEDOM
Not outside of YOU

Sometimes When I Smile

Sometimes when I smile it is because I had
  a perfect encounter with love
Whenever I need her,
  she is always right there waiting;
    right there arms wide open
Sometimes when I smile it is because my soul has no use for tears
Tears can be found in so many places
They have no prejudice
They do not select from the best of us nor do they
  cast lots for the worst of us
My soul has had his fill of tears, but he won't always
  abide with tears
So sometimes when I smile it is because my soul had
  a perfect encounter with love
And she won't have me to leave her in sadness

I See You

You comprehend the words I don't speak
My silence
Speaking volumes into your void
        when my touch become lips
                and your heart listens with purpose
When I count stars in my mind passing time just to sit next to you
Dying to live in your skin
Living to die in your arms
        when my soul become like the wind
                and the wind caresses your skin
When my love spoke evoking smiles and you stared into my eyes
And I spoke never giving time to words that might break you
And I sang then you closed your eyes
        and we found love among the company of our own souls
Reducing my complexity to the singularity of everything that I am,
        finding that you and I is a lie
                for you are me and that's one
So when I reached to the inception of my soul and pulled words from my nonexistence it was you that spoke Love to me from your fingers' tips,
        touching lightly my lips,
                awakening my void through the glory of our singular self
Was it I who found you or you me?
Does it really matter?

No Song in Naked Trees

Where your tips meet my skin
Your lips searching my covering
Breaking my soul you seep within

You are my beautiful peace
My troubled mind you put to sleep
Making love outside these sheets
But the couch is our place
Where you lie on my lap cheek resting on my face
        and I hold you as though you were my soul
        and death came knocking

Do you understand the message in my hand?
Do you know I count the lines in your skin
        etching in my soul what I will picture when I can't see the picture?

I paid attention to the song you played to convey deeply setting feelings;
        listening as though I had demons
        and David played you

No one can sing you
No song can tell me what your eyes say each time I stare in them reading
Do you know I see your walls?

Do you know I wish to paint them
        so you'll know there are beautiful things on the outside waiting?
I will test Patience's patience
Patiently waiting
        till you break free from old hurt feelings
        and spread those worn out wings in Love's wind
I will be your wind
So tell me, where is it you wish to go?

Should I

Should I lose my wings because I fell for you
I'd ask not for a single feather
    but welcome the manifestation of Love's deepest desire

Should I listen to the trees
    when the wind becomes playful with their leaves
    and hear no song
I'd lie beneath your touch until heaven sung
    and our souls slow danced until time grew frail

Should I dive deep inside of you;
    where no eyes have seen,
        no fingers have touched
            and no unhealthy words spoken
I'd inhale one last time everything you ever gave
    relieving myself of this dying flesh
        that I may live forever in heaven's dream,
            here in this sinful world

Whispers of Inspiration

Start being the person today you want people to remember tomorrow.

Rise

Why regard the habitation of the dead
    you daunted soul with watering eyes?
Built them not walls of the sweetest lies?
Words spoken in your heart now forsaken
And your walls shook before time's testing
But it's time you rise!

Fortress bricks carefully placed in the arms not your place
Your rostrum of strength slowly erased
Now you stand declaring to be strong
    as the walls come tumbling
The tears in your eyes as molten clouds come falling
But it's time you rise!

Give attention to the birthplace of the stars
Surmount this pile of brokenness heralding your magnificent rising
Listen to the voice that declares your calling
And when the rivers in your eyes drown your smiles
Wipe them!
For it's time you rise!

Make clear your vision
Script in your mind the reason for this decision
Love has its ways always risking your heart's devastation
But the journey of your story ends not with this situation
So smile at yourself!
Be your biggest fan!
And when the curtains fall give yourself a standing ovation!
Rise!
Applaud yourself until who you've become finds who you were
    and brings back the best part of the show
For it's time you rise!

Do not fear the blackness of the night
The moon's face is your light
Take no thought of the days to come
Because tonight finds death, but tomorrow brings the new Sun
So rise like the morning comes
Rise like the rising sun
Regard not the habitation of the dead
Raise your head and rise instead!
For it is time you rise!

Never underestimate or undermine what you have inside of you to contribute positively to our world. It doesn't matter how large or small you think your contribution is, it is still your contribution and no one else can offer it. The creative power of God is as much in you as it is in anyone else, but only you have the key to unlock that power. Big or small your slice of the cake of life is still your slice and the cake will never be whole without it. So whatever it is that you have passion for pursue it, but always believe in yourself and be true to yourself.

Unbreakable

Why do you believe so strongly that you can break me?
I have slept beneath the open skies
I have warmed the cold touch of naked concrete
  when the moon bathed in her sea of stars
I have heard sounds rising from my stomach
  sending tremors to the core of my soul,
  yet not a single hand of kindness stretched out
So tell me, why do you believe so strongly that you can break me?

To the sun's face I am well acquainted
My dark wrinkled skin testifies
The moon has witnessed my weeping eyes
  more times than I care to remember
I keep my own company from January to December
I have walked among friends and
  met my fiercest foes hidden behind them
With many I have spoken, digesting words void of love
So tell me, why do you believe so strongly that you can break me?

I have not met love in the things time permit me to remember,
  but hatred guise in love-filled words I have seen all my days
When pain raped me of pride and
  fear clutched its cold hands around me
I cried out in a multitude of deaf souls, because no one heard me
You have seen me a time or two,
  maybe twenty,
  exasperated and lonely
  but you spared not one word
I have communed with demons
  sharing the once sacred essence of my body with those unworthy
They took all that I gave
And they were filled, but I rose up empty

So please tell me, why do you believe so strongly that you can break me?

My mother tried, but my father forsook me when I needed him most
In dark rooms hiding from myself I've composed tear-soaked prayers
    sending messages to God,
    walking out with as many answers as I entered with
Still here I am standing weakly strong in the center of your troubled soul
You say you will break me
    and so it is I stand,
    a mirror reflecting everything you hate about yourself;
    everything you lack the courage to be, I am
So please tell me
Why do you believe so strongly, that you can break me?

If God sends you into the kingdom the King can't overlook you forever. Remember that all phases of life have a time and a place. Just because you are in the place doesn't mean the time is right. So be patiently strong in your current position with great expectations.

Brand New Day

I don't know what lies ahead
  but I will leave behind the remains of the dead
Face set to the rising sun
  as visions shed the cover of night
  and courage become a reliable companion

Thoughts of tomorrow bring excitement and fear,
  but I must take myself away from here
I am a slave to this open road,
  enchanted by the sweet whispers of what comes after
I knew friends, but how lonely this road has become
And though teary-eyed and broken, I'm going

The sweet taste of a familiar yesterday
  invading thoughts of an unknown tomorrow,
  but one step less I'll take not
The old me you can have that
My mind is my way out of the misery
My thoughts are wings
  and mountains are pebbles tossed in the wind as I take flight

Time turns as the road winds
  and memories intertwine thinking back on better times
Storms of change provoked seas of confusion
  and my soul had no anchor,
  but "Peace!" I said and briefly it all became still
I had peace in the arms of yesterday,
  but she's grown old and my troubles remain
So though teary-eyed and broken, I'm going

Dark clouds and blue skies convey the same message
  as my broken soul looks to heaven

My prayers don't form as they once did
 but God still listens I'd imagine
Discretions weigh me down;
 tired to the bone as sweat streams down my face here on this lonely road
My thoughts confront me alone in my head,
 but I'm praying sustaining fleeting hope

I've got to take myself away even though there seems no way out
I've searched
I've cried aloud when I couldn't see pass the water in my eyes
The clouds' melting hid my tears
And my voice couldn't penetrate the downpour
 as words lodged themselves in my throat
Baptized in the lies I told myself
 convincing myself truth is what I make of it

I stared into my tear-filled eyes seeing my broken soul
He smiled back a second or two
So there is yet hope walking this lonely road on tomorrow's eve
So I'm tired
And I'm broken, but I'm going

My feet are led by visions I've had of you
You watered my thirsty soul when I needed you
You embraced me till my sins were no more
So with hope I come
Dreams of you keeping alive a heart that desires death
But my face is set to the rising sun
With thoughts reflecting tomorrow's provisions as visions become clear
 and courage a reliable companion
I'm teary-eyed and I'm broken, but I'm still going
Tomorrow, I'm coming

If you expect everyone to support your vision you've already lost sight of your purpose. From time to time you're going to carry something inside of you that is not for everyone. Stop going around trying to find people to father your purpose. Your purpose is a divine seed planted inside the womb of your determination. Unless you wish to abort, never stop pursuing your purpose. You do not need everyone to co-sign your vision. When those who are not with you walk away from you they will take everything that you have vested in them though it was never theirs to have. Protect your passion. Don't share your vision with everyone.

Letter on Your Mirror

These thoughts of mine are not of here
In fact, I don't belong here,
  but I've been here so long I'm starting to look and smell like you
If only you knew how badly I want to fly away, to be free
I will never get used to this shit
When the noise is turned up I'm right there with you
The pleas within are drowned out,
  but when the music stops,
  when I'm alone with just me again,
  I can hear everything
I hear that beautiful voice trapped within begging me "please take me away"
So one day I will release myself
One day I will allow these wings to grow
One day I will allow them take my soul away,
  because he's just too tired of it all
You should know I'm completely disloyal to you
I want nothing to do with you
  and this path takes me away from the bed we use to lie in;
  so I'll stay faithful to the call away from it all
I hate the fact that you're there every step of the way,
  but I suppose it must be this way, at least for today
God knows I pray for a fork in this road every day
I pray especially hard on those days when I have to look at your face
  and listen to the rubbish that comes out of your mouth
Rest assured, God willing this road splits,
  it will be the very last you see of me
And don't take my picture
In fact, don't remember anything about me
Don't speak of me
  because I would hate to leave my name on such filthy lips
Just one thing, if you wish I will gladly take a kiss,
  but only if it's the one which says goodbye

Refusing to see the greatness inside you is a false sense of humility. You will never be able to live up to your highest potential until you recognize and accept your highest potential. The greatness inside you is the greatness of God who created you; to live up to it is to honor God. Likewise to downplay your potential is to place limitations on the limitless nature of God. So I dare you, be bold enough to see the greatness locked up inside you even when no one else does because it is pointless to die when you haven't really lived.

All the Pretty Things Fade

The beauty within her song implores his soul's attention,
    but her words broke his heart before the final note was sung
The mystery of love, how two souls connect beyond flesh
Lives perfectly intertwine, they bargain with death
She inhales and he knows life,
    but all the pretty things fade as her smile grows distant

Mother's love reminds him
    indeed there is a God
    whose essence is the purest love
Always trust Him she said
Then she breathed out and walked with them
He cried
He questioned
He found comfort inside his head
But days he remembered sitting beside her bed
Can you still hear me?
The silence of the dead
And all the pretty things fade as she walked away

Is it a foolish thing trying to catch the wind?
The feel of tiny fingers touching your skin when a child begs your attention
Can the angry heart give birth to a smile?
Time changes all things, yet time itself never changes
Is change his grand illusion?
Today you find yourself living in yesterday
Yesterday you prayed for tomorrow,
    but tomorrow is death so you choose life reverting to what was
    or stand loyal to what may never be
What is there outside of you and me?
Your soul was his comfort now his madness spreads
And all the pretty things fade as he wipes you from his head

Honey bees build hives on corpses
    while black paint speaks to white canvas, but who sees art?
The lost feasts on confusion though the message is clear
Broken hearts hide behind fake smiles, but does any truly care?
My thoughts will drive you mad lest you've been there
You see shadows never tell the full story, so step into my light
The door remains open though I haven't been visited in a while
Don't be afraid
Within you'll find life or death,
    but either way you'll find glory if you seek truth
But please hurry because all the pretty things fade

If you hear God calling your name why would you turn to people and answer? Purpose is divine. You can't find it in people. Just wait for God to start calling your name and watch how many people will talk about you. Great people are not the ones not talked about. Great people are the ones who know better than to get distracted by fruitless chatter. BELIEVE in yourself. You seek higher things because you have a higher purpose. Weeds must and will be weeds. Yes weeds have purpose too, but their purpose isn't to surround roses; so don't be that Rose caught among them wondering why you can't bloom.

Flight of the Caged Bird

When my wings spread open
cast my shadow against the wind
and set me free
Take these bars away from me
and I - will - fly
I will perch in the giants of forests
I will sing in the choirs of autumn's colors
Let blue skies cry
washing away the weight of my sin,
making lighter the burden of the wind
This graceful first flight,
soaring carelessly naked from the cold of the night
Onward to dawn's destiny
for she awaits me where our mother gives birth to the new sun
warming my pale skin
If only you could see from God's eyes
I've watched tearless clouds play in the purposeful wind
And it all felt familiar,
but I am a stranger
A caged wanderer
A virgin to the sound of my soul's song
waking mountains' peaks at the dawn of new life

I will wash my stain of fear in the ocean's soul
Remembering days spent in that cage of old
when freedom was uncharted territory
Now surely seeing freedom clearly
My mended wings dance in the invisible wind

I enchant myself
I am in love with myself
because freedom gave me reason

to see my beautiful soul hidden deeply
I smile in the bright glare of the rising sun
closing my eyes taking in everything
I hear thunders' mighty voices trumpeting the breaking of my chains
I hear songbirds singing to the glory of the spring from which my
dying soul bloomed
The valiant rainbow proudly mans the gateway of my paradise
And how beautiful the expression of emotions
beyond those bars of depression
How sweet the tears of a renewed heart among those divinely set apart
I am among my kind,
lost in the mind that knows no confinement
Among the free,
anticipating the day these thoughts will shed fear
setting free the caged bird inside of me

Your thoughts are paint. Your mouth is a brush. When you speak you paint your reality. To paint freedom or imprisonment is entirely up to you. Limit yourself in your thoughts and you will live a limited life. Creativity is locked up inside of you. So create your world. Speak it into existence.

Swords, Cords & Spiritual Poems

Life's canvas white
On this canvas write, casting all fears
Master your brush
Live in the stroke
Leave your mark
Embellishing this beautiful existence

You are fruitful, so multiply
Know your calling
Answer to nothing less
I'm the wordsmith melting sacred thoughts shaping destiny
I'm the warrior skilled in his art, perfectly perfecting imperfections
Slicing doubt to pieces taking lives
    giving life to dead souls

Now come, take your portion
Fabricated from remains, rising like vapor
My soul is immune to snares
Breaking spells, casting spells without potions
Resistance is futile so please release yourself of whatever notion
    birthed such thoughts within
The moon knew the ocean raising tides,
    she gave birth,
    my inception
Of truth I'm familiar with the deep
I opened my mouth letting the heart speak
Now light has come
He spoke life
Dried bones, dead bones, He spoke life
Speaking releasing demons setting free your captive soul
Setting at ease your troubled thoughts

Light shone in dark places
Consciousness eradicates ignorance
Eyes slowly blink taking picture, reading scripture
My pen ordained an apostle spreading this gospel
Sight given to the blind
Life is written among the stars,
    yesterday,
        today
            and tomorrow
Speaking prophetically poetically He said my touch healed
    tomorrow's sorrows

So tune your cords to my vibration fusing sweet music
    with a perfect moment
Take all that I am
Have everything I will be
All that I desire you must be
Breathe this fresh air and learn of me
Sit quietly, relax and breathe slowly
Follow this flow
    my seducing tempo
        as I sing sweetly for your soul
Your destiny awaits, yet destiny is
There is no destiny just the passion of this moment passing on the wind
There is no tomorrow so don't be afraid of tomorrow,
    of the emptiness that is the unknown

Create! Dirty your canvas and create
Take sips of this art I make creating love
Watch my stroke as I capture time
Mixing potions of the heart, you were mine from the very start
    when I breathed love into your lifeless heart
The spirit knows not death
    so I took your life through fire removing impurities,
        revealing the greatness locked within

Look at me and see yourself
I am not, this image it is you
Now breathe!
Inhale me
Exhale all that I am not
Breathe!
Inhale me
Watch your stroke, allow it to take you captive
Be his slave
Create your life
This canvas, do not leave it white
It is ours to have this life, so be brave,
    breathe slowly and whatever you do,
    never cease to write

Don't be so lost in someone else's shadow that you miss the chance to cast your own. Your purpose is as important as anyone else's. There is nothing wrong with appreciating someone else's story, but if you don't tell your own who will be there to appreciate it? Don't rob someone the chance to be inspired by your life.

Dirt from Broken Vase

(Inspired by the life of Jean-Michel Basquiat)
Trapped in darkness,
then darkness became my light
They tried covering my eyes,
instead they gave me sight
I've wanted freedom,
but solitary confinement told me things about myself that made me feel beautiful;
things that made me worthy to walk among the rejected
Still, I walk alone
Now I see myself without seeing myself
Feeling comfort among my lonely thoughts
And the canvas portraying my story is never more intricately painted,
but time ages
Time ages
How much time have I left?
My time is expiring
My light slowly fades
If I now grow wings will I fly?
Will I fly?
I want to fly
I want to fly to His light that I may see myself outside of myself
But I am afraid to see what I think I am
Don't take my life
Not now when I am ready to fly
Not now when I am ready to fly
I've seen the light
It's no longer dark
They no longer cover my eyes
Please take my sight
Don't let me see
My wings slowly grow with aging time

Don't let me be
I am not ready to fly
I am not ready to fly, but time ages
So I am going to fly
My wings aren't fully grown
But I am going to fly

Eagles don't take flight lessons from chickens.

Know who you are. Know what you are capable of. Be the eagle you were created to be. Mountains are there to show you the strength of your wings so stop listening to naysayers and soar above those mountains.

Whispers of **My Mother**

These pieces were all inspired by my mother, the beautiful Hyacinth Brown. Mother you are a wise, beautiful and loving soul. I still remember your quiet spirit and that smile that could warm the coldest of hearts. These pieces I dedicate to you, with the purest love.

One night, while in college, I stayed up the entire night doing homework. At about 6:30 AM in the morning my mother woke up to get ready for work. She saw light coming from beneath my bedroom door and curiously opened the door. I turned around and looked at her and she looked at me, but neither one of us said anything before she proceeded to closing the door. A few days later she said to me **"When you reach where you are going in life don't let anyone make you feel guilty about your success because I've seen how hard you've worked for i**t." My mother knew something that I needed to know and that is why she spoke those words into my life. Over the years I've met a few people who tried to make me feel bad about my accomplishments in life, but I've always kept those words from my mother close to heart.

People who do not mean you well will never take the time to learn about your path in this life. They do not know where you are coming from. They do not know how hard you worked to get where you are. However, these same people will never miss an opportunity to throw your success in your face because they failed themselves in one way or another. I thank my mother eternally for those words of empowerment and I leave those words with you. **DO NOT EVER allow anyone to make you feel guilty about your success. Be proud of who you are. Be proud of what you have accomplished. There is no reason under the sun for you to feel bad about what you have or who you are when by the sweat of your brow you are eating your bread.**

Healer

In purple fields of Hyacinth I search for my heart's darling
In recollection I see everything; warm tears from her eyes falling
Then death fell in love with her and stole my everything

Briefly my mind left me
    but I hid it,
    her freedom's key,
    in thoughts only God can see
Then I wrote her poem among constellations
Every line written revealing a painfully beautiful memory
My words they freed her
I gave her wings to the winds,
    but my soul wouldn't have her to be a passenger of the wind
So I wrote again,
    breaking again her mended wings

In my dreams,
    her spirit's dwelling,
    softly she spoke, whispering;
    then I awoke but she wasn't there
Once I stood between the worlds,
    listening to the song of the trees
    when the wind played her symphony
    and leaves danced soothing me
I knew you were there
    because I heard the whisper of love
    when my name departed your lips
    echoing through the bedlam of my mind

I am trying to decipher the meaning of your coming
Trying to understand what it is you're saying
    in the consistency of the imagery

and the strong presence of your invisible soul
One night I saw your broken wings mended
then set free
when through the window of life's parallel your sparrow flew
until I saw you no more
So he wept,
your healer
and wrote beautifully from his heart

When life is passing you by stop her. Converse for a while. Laugh for a while because behind her is death and he'll stop to talk even when you don't want to speak.

Hyacinth's Flower

At times I wonder what life would be like without you
Well, just try to imagine the earth without her oceans,
    the trees without their leaves
        or the heavens without a single star
You are my tower of strength
I sit sometimes recalling all you have done
If ever I was hurt you would drop the world and tend to my pain
I have seen your trials and heard your frustrations
I have seen your tears and heard the cries that rose from your soul
I remember when you were at your lowest
You barely had strength to sit upright,
    but still you found the strength to uplift me
"I don't want you to fret", that is what you said so selflessly

When the world forsakes me I know you never will
I don't think God has given me a greater gift
So I will treasure you in this life and the next
I will be there if ever you need someone just to sit next to you
I will sit a lifetime if you need me to
Besides that of God, I have not known a greater love
You don't speak much, but I know you bear some heavy burdens
    and well mom, I will help you carry them now
I endeavor to do whatever it takes to see that beautiful smile on your face
I think of it and it makes me smile
You are so beautiful to me, so beautiful
I love you beyond words… beyond time.

Acceptance of the past is requisite to the successful pursuit of a meaningful future.

The Day the Night Ate the Sun

Wake up mom…
I am afraid
Listen to the prayers filling the room
They pray for you
Mom I know you hear me
I know you feel my tears falling on your face
Mom, wake up!
I know I said go if you were too tired to stay,
    but what do I know anyway?
I know your skin is now a prison
    and freedom is God's voice whispering softly inside your soul,
    but I am afraid
Please don't go
Please, move a finger
Just a simple sign
Just a tiny squeeze
Your hand is in mine
Mom, breathe!
Breathe mom…
Breathe!
Mom!
Mom!
Mom

Kind hearts are not unfamiliar with pain, but a kind heart has no price for men to pay. Hence it is far better to have a kind heart than all the riches in the world.

Where Love Lies

A mound of dirt and cut flowers mark the place where love lies
Runaway tears leave tracks on broken faces
    and children's hearts weep fearfully
    accepting the tangibility of their reality

Unable to breathe though the wind is so soft
Unable to hear though watch birds sing so beautifully
Mama sleeps with the angels now
    and I envy the heavens' gift of the best love

Quietly I knelt,
    pouring my heart's secrets into the hot earth
    like water invading porous soil
Mama, can you hear me?
A still silence penetrates my hope,
    reminding me that death consumes voices too
Still I wait hoping time will change its mind and undo what has been done

But the days carry on
    and the nights tease with glimpses of her in lucid dreams
Twice she was dying,
    once I saved her,
    then I rouse from my sleep,
    but she did not

Mama, do you see me?
Her picture stares back with piercing eyes
    conveying last words reminding me of better times
    when she spoke, "I love you baby"
    and I replied "I love you too"

You poured from your beautiful soul until you had nothing left,

then God showed mercy
and I cried bitterly
You're gone, but I still go hoping against hope answers I'll find
Conversing with mommy seeking some peace of mind
Kneeling on the flattened mound replenishing dead lilies with dying roses
Pouring words through hardened dirt
while the uncut grass dances slowly beneath me
Mama, do you still love me?

Never take a perfect moment in time for granted. We are all familiar with days we wish never came, but such is a part of the journey of life. Now and again, however, we encounter a perfect moment in time. Maybe that moment when you realize the love someone has for you. Maybe a perfect kiss from someone that makes your heart smile. Maybe a perfect moonlit sky on a first date. Maybe the words "I love you" followed by a hug from a child. Maybe dancing to a song you really really love. Maybe laughing hysterically with your best friend. Whatever it is, cherish those moments when they come and be thankful for them.

Looking Forward to Yesterday

A thought floats in the vacancy of my mind
    as a feather in the gentle breeze of the silent soul
Smiles as pure as untainted waters rise when you invade my space
I never imagined we'd have been here today;
    oceans of time between destined souls motivated of love
But the sun still lights the moon across oceans of stars
And I still crave your presence
    because you are still the darling of my time

Daily I paint your portrait within,
    mastering brilliant colors of life and I'm born again
Perfecting my craft I compel words and they resurrect the good days
I still think of that smile that conveyed your love
Tomorrow didn't value you as yesterday did,
    but tomorrow will not have all of me
    because I will come back to yesterday,
    the most beautiful of my days

Every bird has a song to sing, but every bird does not sing for everyone. This is the often unseen beauty of diversity. There is something for everyone. Therefore, enjoy the song of your own bird and do not waste your time telling someone else how badly their bird is out of tune.

Last Song the Sparrow Sung

The sparrow sung her song for the stranger
Her song was so beautiful it made flowers bloom,
    echoed in his room,
    but not one word did he remember
She sang,
    then she cried,
        till finally she died,
            wishing her song was heard by the stranger
One day while tending the garden, the stranger saw something unfamiliar
In the sprouting of every leaf,
    the blooming of every flower,
    the sparrow's song written beautifully for the stranger
The song he will sing forever

God created the Hyacinth with all her beauty, yet many pass her by not having seen her essence. In life many will pass you by not having seen God in you, but God has eyes for you, so have eyes for yourself even when the world passes you by.

Secrets of Night's Ocean

Among the company of stars I am
Beneath the deep blackness of the Moon's ocean
        I have heard secrets my soul won't speak of
A stranger I was in my own head,
        emptying my mind till strength had no part of me
My fight took flight
Then tears streamed down my face
        when I tried to evade my emotions
My thoughts rose like the soul of the dead
They wanted no part of me
I desired the bed of my madness
        though it's comfort never seemed to quiet me
Memories of my mistakes swept over me
        like the waters of a thousand rivers
Enthralled I was by the reflection of a broken man
I searched tirelessly, but couldn't find my song
Then mother's voice spoke in the still silence of my broken heart
"You are still great my son"

Cloud-Soaked Sun

Our conversation sentenced hope to eternal chains
Echoes of anger saturate the moment,
both our eyes revealing this truth
My lips vibrated amidst the turmoil,
but not a word broke through
Silence, my dear friend,
my constant gardener
He visited my garden and my weeds knew the fire

Yesterday butterflies came,
but the sun's rise brought crows the color of the moonless night
Still the lone rose blooms in the soil of confusion
and bless the one whose eyes found a way

Calloused hands say nothing of the softened heart,
but whose patience and gentleness will bring forth the clam's glory?
Staring within
conjuring demons
exorcising myself from myself
I was baptized in lies resurrecting fears
I found companion among the dead
My stay gave reason for celebration
So we laughed pouring libations

Mother was a comfort I knew well
Her touch eased my pain,
but her hands are no more
And what becomes of that?
What becomes of the soul saturated with grief
beneath the cloud-soaked sun?
I run to the embrace I longed for,
but loneliness has never sunk deeper

Whispers of Inner Meditation

Through ignorance I sought God because I feared Hell, but through understanding I seek God because I crave Truth.

Grace

Your inception was of a whisper
Echoing betwixt the mountainous flames of burning stars
How you adjured timeless vibrations
Sweetly singing over my illusory soul when salvation conceived aspirations
In the deep silence of the eyeless darkness,
        I shouted from the high peak of soul-wrenching pain
Patience and persistence were my only friends,
        until you came
        and knew I the purpose of love
My offering was a desolate river's valley
        when her provisions abandoned her for the mysterious deep
But you saw the remnants of my glory
        when my wrinkled skin laid beneath your purposeful lips
My soul you then quickened with a divine kiss
        and I knew life in all its splendor

You found me in my bed of troubles
        when I mounted your comfort
        and anguish grew out of touch
My eyes revealed deep secrets,
        as warm tears seeped into your celestial covering
In my freedom's wake,
        with you I walked among them
        with whom once shared I sacred feelings

How their eyes filled with envy
        knowing not they the quandary from which you saved me
        when I beheld your ethereal beauty
Of all which came in times prior
        death lead them
Sweet death persuaded them,
        but you are the gift of the echoing whisper

piercing the fabric of my mystical essence;
intimate with the purpose of my existence
Walking betwixt the mountainous flames of burning stars
Sweetly singing over my mended pieces
as I esteem you from the mountain of my peace,
heralding your saving Grace

Every word I speak bears witness to my soul. If I speak well, but lack integrity my words will stand to judge, convict and condemn me. If I speak well and walk in the light of integrity my words will stand to uplift, edify and liberate me. The hearts of those that I speak into will echo the things spoken and loud the echo will be. I am grateful for those who have shown me myself through my words.

Lullaby of the Slumbered Soul

If freely I spoke as the wind
        taking no thought of listening trees
My forest would wither in my awakening
The echo of change vibrates deep inside my photon of consciousness
And we are not two you and I
I die because you won't live
I sing loudly for you,
        moving mountains' peaks,
        but your heart stood in death's silence
Awake my soul's keeper
Awake before my song dies inside my throat

I have no competition because those who are on my side are not my competition and those who are on the opposing side are no competition for God.

Reflecting Mirrors

In his darkest hour he revealed the glory of the sun
Embracing love reassuring himself of the newness yet to come
Fear has no place as the void fills speaking his truth
    while I gave my undivided self
Lullabying oceans with truth infecting all life with life through life
He breathed slowly
    and knew the inmost essence of his essence

Lost in the cosmos of his solitary abide,
    waiting to be found
    then myself came
In His presence fear is not
Love has no equal
Am I Him?
Is He me?
Are they us?
Are we them?
Are there any?
Reflection...

Far reached, well detached;
    seeking the pleasures of former feasts when he knew not his fill
They called his name as a mother seeking her child across the
    divide of the living,
    but I gave no answer
He has no desire,
    but his desire gave in to desire
    now I'm stuck in orbit with the former things

An evil word breaking your lips has no loyalty. Yes it will go where you send it, but in due time, like a chicken, it will come home to roost.

Water for the Soul

What is it when my thirsty soul finds itself in the stream of sustenance?
I stare in awe of His glory
Though the light has taken my sight
Letting go I float away on waves of virtue
    allowing this truth to guide my destitute soul
As the me that I was empties,
    slowly I'm filled from the source of what I am to be
We were one before,
    but the rise of the new sun has nothing on me
I watched the growth of the wings by which freedom I will find
I am released from the bondage I knew,
    those old chains of familiarity
I am at peace,
    as the peace one finds when he allows himself to be quieted by the
    whispers of the wind passing through aged leaves
What is it when a thirsty soul finds himself in the stream of truth?
First I must sip,
    only then can I answer

To treat your enemy the way they treat you it is necessary for you to become like your enemy. However, in so doing, you end up with two enemies. For what differentiates one enemy from the next if their actions are the same?

Time's Tale

Passing from the womb to the wind
I welcome the life unknown,
    defying illusions of fear
I am the kind of Love
The kind Time's Tale speaks lovely of
So leave me to crooked paths
    where battered dreams find charming memories
    because my eyes know well the darkness of Life,
    so stumble I will not
Before you, I was
Inside of you, I am
You are no more, yet I am
The invisible visible wind of change
The secrets of Time's Tale
The womb of all things pure
    reclaiming stars casted from the birthplace of gods
And shifting sands tell Time's Tales when old things are anew
Let her Tales take you
She's seen places and comforted hearts innumerable
So rest well, in Time's Tale
Where silent voices echo in the heart willing to hear

God placed Creation on His mind and spoke it into existence. You were created in the likeness of God; so be careful what you set your mind on. Be careful what you speak from your lips. What you create in your inner world will eventually manifest itself in your physical existence. So before you speak it make certain you are ready to receive it.

Breath of Life

Who Am I?
I am a thought of Creation
The manifestation of Perfection
    when void places rebuked darkness
    and truth conceived wisdom
I gave birth to time,
    but how the fruit receives praise
    when the tree stands before the elements forgotten
Subjected to fear,
    caged among the broken,
    I've conjured the fallen
    perpetuating my descent into the belly of ignorance
    where sweet songs pacify the regression of love
And God spoke of my inception in a time not yet my own,
    but the long and tedious journey circles back home
    and mother is waiting

They searched me out
I am found,
    but questions will not have their hearts to find rest
Would a flower evade the sun when darkness embodies death?
I'll have no part in confusion;
    not when understanding seeps through my being
    like the wind through naked trees
I am Love
The only Love you will never know
I am the fear provoking your weary eyes when moons rise
But you will not have me,
    thus your void continues to deepen
    when I've delivered you from the snare of your unfruitful imagination
What am I?
What am I not?

Hold your speech and speak not words to defy the rising of the Son
Your relentless efforts are time wasted endeavoring to tear down
where you have not built
My wings sing silencing the sound of ten thousand eagles in flight
My soul shines to the shame of the sun,
but he craves death though life desperately cries out his name
Have you begun to see?
I am the flight of the butterfly when the wind converses with its wings
and places unknown summon the grace of its presence

The Creation is like an art studio filled with diverse pieces of interestingly beautiful art. Find the piece that steals your attention, but do not ridicule the piece that captures mine. To ridicule what I find beautiful is to ridicule the artist who blessed us with this beautiful gallery. Rest assured, there are innumerable pieces, but one artist. How grateful we should be that He took the time to create something for everyone. So enjoy the beauty within diversity. Enjoy that which steals your heart and please leave me to indulge myself in that which captures mine.

Bedlam

Noise
Everything is noise
Soul wrenching vibrations stirring my otherwise stilled troubles
I seek a quiet place their voices aren't heard
Deep inside of you,
  where your beautiful thoughts soothe my turmoil
Deciphering prayers,
  intercepting cries for my own redemption
My thoughts create and destroy me in the same instance
Inception and death fused sharing one place in time eternal
  when Light has no place with Darkness
Then how can I be?
Truth defied
Truth deprived of my undivided self
My psychosis begin the metamorphosis of what I was supposed to be
My desires lie beyond my purpose,
  but purpose is a disciplinary selfishly having its way
But I'll perpetuate the rebellion until time have its way

Glimpses of light
Glimpses of truth
Evading the inevitability of my madness
I see glimpses of you
A smile breaks the gloom as spring rains meeting fertile ground,
  life anew the day I met you
Wanting to give you my all
Wondering if I have anything left
But the little that the poor has…
I digress

Your heart bears frustrations, it needs to beat
My mind is snared in confusion, it needs to speak

Of the two comes the inception of one
Two souls composing the same song
    singing loudly to the deafened audience,
    but I hear you
Do you hear me?
I speak sacred things though not heard, not by them
My thoughts inhale the vibrations of your heart's meditations
Now be the place of my rest
That my soul may sleep in beautiful peace
My cage lies open, but freedom is the clipped wings of the captive born
I need time,
    and time for the time it will take because I must take my time,
    at least that would be wise this time
But by reason of fear my thoughts are confined
    in a place where freedom reigns
So gently, take my madness and silence this noise

The further you dive into God the more amazing He becomes. Sometimes you have to go through some stuff, but everything you endure reveals more of His infinite mercies. Imagine God is the ocean and you are a drowning soul. You do not have to search for God; simply realize that He is and that you are in the midst of Him. Once you realize this you simply relax, you stop the futile struggle to survive and His goodness keeps you afloat.

Serenity

Trapped inside serenity
There is no desire for freedom
No need of salvation
Losing sight of reality
Having nothing at all
    and no room to contain it all
The smell of fresh leaves took my soul captive
Imprisoned by serenity,
    then thoughts of you eluded me
The power of your words now broken
A love greater than yours has shown me everything
I cannot break free
But still I'm fighting
Trapped inside serenity
Lost, and yet found

Knowledge empowers you to shape the situation.

Ignorance empowers the situation to shape you.

Blind Seeker

You construct a fortress of lies to accommodate your unwillingness
to accept truth
Misunderstanding the simplicity of basic necessity
you proliferate doctrines of plenteous portions
decorating your container of bones
The raging flame dowsed
Reduced to a flicker because the divine purpose is of far more
significance than the survival of the eternal you
You have missed the mark
Your destiny recreated in the finite illusions of the fool
You do not see the essence of who you are
And misunderstanding of self is the greatest tragedy

If you need those around you to acknowledge that which makes you great before you understand your greatness you may die blind to your own brilliance. Know yourself, acknowledge, support and love yourself; even when you are your only fan.

Perspective

If I was never hungry I would've never known God provides
If I was never sick I would've never known God heals
If I was never angry I would've never known God grants peace
If I was never lonely I would've never known God is a friend
If I never cried I would've never known God comforts the broken

In the valley I cry for the hill
On the hill I thank God for taking me through the valley
If I was never in the valley I would never have reason to thank
    God for the mountain
Thus, in all things, I give thanks

Allow God to bless you. You deserve it. You cried when everything grew dark so He sent light. So open your eyes and receive new life. Do not feel guilty about it. Do not allow anyone to make you feel guilty. Just receive it and be thankful.

Supplications of a Misplaced Soul

If I could remove the soiled portions of my heart
I would go back again to that place where my soul knew no
    separation from perfection
I would go back and undo my every evil deed,
    but I cannot,
    and the fact remains, evil deeds have not seen the last of me
In time, when I deem the value of this rotting flesh more precious
    than that of the divine self I will partake of them again
I will cry again
My soul will weep again
I will dirty myself again after being made the like of snow
This flesh is my portion
There is no escaping that,
    but my will is strong and my resolve to be
    light is etched in the fabric of no time
If you will have me, I can be the very best of me again
Just teach me
Show me myself
Show me how and I will fall in love with the very best of me again
Till death I will not part,
    but before death I so desperately need your help,
    because I don't really know where to start

The rose that wishes to be a lily commits two great evils. One, it denies great pleasure to those who love the smell of the rose. Two, it turns a blind eye to its divine purpose.

Song of the Broken Mind

This pain is an illusionist in my mind
    creating a scene so far from Truth it has no place amongst my desires,
    yet the superficiality of it all soothes my troubled soul
I often cry asking you to show me your face amidst the madness
I now ask, "How could I have not known?"
But I know now that time had not yet completed her work
I know now
My consciousness is awake
My understanding is conversant with Light
    but darkness lurks,
    tugging at my soul
    as I fill this void with the void outside of you
Do not show me your face because your face I have seen
    and your appearance is no stranger to me
Rather teach me to recognize your face in the midst of the noise
It is the remedy of my fears
My fears thrive in your absence
Free me from these fears
Restore my courage and teach me to recognize your face
This day is bigger than I
It has brought burdens I can't bear
Watch my feet tremor beneath the unbalanced weight
    and there is none to stand with me
I have known the sun
He has shown me all things,
    but my eyes prove useless when he hides his face from me
Darkness grows and I am alone
My fears thrive because I do not recognize your face
This one request I have,
    the one desire that now fills my heart;
    before this darkness departs,
    before the sun should chase these fears away;

teach me to recognize your face in the midst of this madness
that the sun shall not have glory in my praise

I searched for a leader worth following, but there were none to be found so I stepped out facing the sun with my shadow behind me. It is natural for you to want to follow someone. The greatest among us, our most notable leaders, were once followers, but sometimes good leaders are not easily found. When there is no one left worth following it means it's time for you to lead; even if you are your only follower.

Revelations of Self Love

You read me, but you do not understand the simplicity of this truth
We converse, but you do not give your undivided self
We danced, the song has ran its course, but you are still moving
You are still moving

Complicatedly simple I am, but isn't everything?
Complexity is the unknown in the ignorant mind
But I have shown you all things
I have spoken it
I have written it
I have painted the most beautiful work of the brush and its canvas,
  but what is color to the blind?

So forgive me
Forgive everything about me that irritates your existence
Forgive the love I embrace that sets fire in your skin
Forgive my words of encouragement;
  words which pierce the thickest darkness;
  words purposed to liberate you from yourself
I meant no harm, but the afflictions of your heart has
  brought a deeply set confusion;
  now you deceive yourself thinking it is I that you hate
The truth is, it is yourself that you can't bear to
  share the same room with
You project the ugliness of yourself towards me,
  but darkness cannot elude itself
So there you are still confused,
  still perplexed,
  still trying to shed yourself,
  only to reveal more of the ugliness that you have become

But I love you!

I love you because I see the essence of who you are
So I embrace time, because she has kept me
She has shown me her faithfulness
She has shown me the glory you have yet to become

You are beautiful,
    if only you could see,
    but you deprive yourself seeking ways to break me
Save yourself
Save your strength
My life is not yours to have,
    but I await you in a time not yet our own
Take your time though
I'm in no hurry

Sometimes when you are stranded in the sea of indecision God will send a storm to wash you to the shore of your destiny. The storms of life are not always sent to destroy you. Sometimes they are sent to deliver you. If you will only have faith and endure the rough seas the day will come when you will sit on that beautifully calm beach of destiny, looking back out at sea and saying, "I made it."

Emptiness

Emptiness is my portion, my meat of sustenance
I am awake yet asleep because my soul has grown somnolent
I dwell in the heights,
    but as a wandering man of no possessions
    I spend the entirety of my days in this valley of desolation
I am from a time and a place not my own,
    thus I trot in this valley of apportioned time unwelcomed;
    the portion bequeathed me by the hand unknown
I am in need of my Lord
My soul cries from the depths of his rest
Solitude, my unwelcomed confidant,
    I receive you with much disinclination
Yet! I trust, and my soul does eat of the bread of true faith
    knowing that in time the time I have been allotted will be no more;
    the time of my purpose will manifest itself as the long awaited
    sun breaking his eastern point of procession
I will receive it well
    as the husbandman receives his bride in the day of his nuptial

---

The selfish man abhors his own soul for no man can taste true love when his is the only reflection he sees when glancing into the spiritual waters of life. To love perfectly is to be completely freed from the bonds of selfishness.

Familiar Stranger

Why am I misunderstood when I have
opened the door to the inner me?
I have shown you the light within,
yet you are perplexed in the face of my truth
You do not understand when I cry sacred things in the morning
We lie at rest, but our souls know not union
Digest my words and learn of me as they are the
manifestations of the meditations within the heart
Commune with me
Sit at my table and allow our souls to converse taking delight in the
knowledge of the higher things
Is it my love for you that has drawn you near
or rather your love for me?
Is it compassion that compels you
or do you move with the catalyst of selfishness?
You are satisfied with fleshly things
I have eating my fill thereof;
yet the sounds bellowing from my soul speaks of a man with an
insatiable appetite
I seek a deeper truth, a more satisfying truth
I seek true bread
because only a fool knows his fill at the table of stones

The path of truth thirsts for the soles of the feet of men. Those who seek truth will find themselves with an abundance of questions, but very few, if any true answers. Those who seek truth are like the wind because they are indeed born of the Spirit. They cannot be contained and they will not find rest until they have found their purpose.

Gratitude

I woke up from my tormented rest
        and rain clouds hovered above my soul
But God! I said…
Father thank you for the source of water
        because my soul thirsted and my strength was almost gone

I drew memories from places deeply secreted
        and my eyes flooded because of them
But God! I said…
Father thank you for showing me that my heart is still yet tender
        because I had faced times tough enough to make me grow cold

Today I turned to you, my friend
I saw that you no longer held a sacred place for me inside of you
But God! I said…
Father thank you for showing me my enemies hidden in my sacred place
        because I thought I had someone to confide in
        and so I almost shared my heart with my foe

I felt a pressure I was not familiar with
I was uncertain how I should have handle myself in the depth
But God! I said…
Father thank you for giving me a reason to have faith again
        because I remembered the days you raised me up
        when all hope seemed lost

I found a friend tired and weakened from her burdens
Bitterly she cried
But God! I said…
Father thank you for the opportunity to be one with my humanity
        because I reveled in my sunny days for so long
        I'd almost forgotten the ones drowning in the dark

Never tell your dreams to those who lack vision.

They'll just give you reasons to wake up.

Coming Forth by Day

I am regarded as one opposed to the force guiding curious souls
    along the path of truth to that inner self of divine origin
Walking the intricate pathways of my own mind,
    in my own darkness
I am searching for the origin of that Light,
    but it is no easy task and of certain
    no path for the weak at heart
The darkness is thick and deep,
    but out of the darkness we attain the greatest vibrations of light
    though blind eyes see not
What am I?
A question I've both deliberated and evaded in the same thought
And denial of self is the greatest sin;
    as such, the cup of my transgression flows over unto itself
But Truth is the darling of my soul
    though I converse with charming lies in my lonesomeness
    all the days she has gone away from me
I long to hold her,
    to be intimate,
    to taste of her true essence to my soul's contentment
But she is not easily found,
    by reason of her encapsulation by mistruths,
    by those who will not search her out until life is no more
As for me, I am hungry
    and of no other breast comes my sustenance;
    so search I must
For I am as the unseen wind among colorful trees
    dancing among leaves of many kind;
    seeking my place among the stars
    though it frets my heart when I consider the matter of my nonexistence
So tell me, am I worthy?

A place I find among them,
    among many,
    yet stand I in solitude as a man without knowledge of self
Balance is the principal thing if it is I am to not dichotomize self and truth;
    for the two is one as the rainbow is not many
The sun is not always high in the sky nor
    does the moon have glory always among those
    who crave her when night falls
Because purpose knows its place
    and abides not outside the confines of its season
And though convoluted,
    I know it is not void of purpose,
    this existence of mine
Hence my soul searches relentlessly until the day my cup is finally emptied
Where I once feared,
    the darkness mistakenly swallowed me up
    revealing to me its hidden truths
    and the mystery is no more
Where I walked aimlessly, purpose is now a lamp unto my feet
Where I fought ten thousand enemies,
    I now fight one
    striking mighty blows
    yet it is I who hemorrhage
    being the victor and the victim of the same battle
But who am I?
A question I've both deliberated and evaded in the same thought

---

When you are ready to give birth to your purpose you will find a stumbling block in every other endeavor.

Spoken Word

Between words I am naked
yet beautifully clothed
imprisoned
yet willfully free
I am at HOME
in my WORLD
Having total control over who I choose to let in
And you!
You are most welcomed
in my loud silence
but slowly whisper that I may be enthralled
by every word spoken

Have you ever had someone tell you what they think of you and it made you second guess what YOU thought of yourself? That is called a seed sown. Don't water it. It will grow. Don't allow your identity to live in the minds of people who do not know your purpose nor wish to see you succeed at it. The more you think about what they say the more you will believe it. In time you will become their creation instead of God's creation. In time you will carry out what they will you to do instead of what God created you to do. No one knows you better than you know yourself; so if it's not God don't allow anyone to tell you who you are, what you are or what you are capable of doing.

Mind's Song

Freedom!
Freedom is your womb of inception
Conceived of the DNA of the cosmos
        there is not a place or a time to hold you
You have not a name they can enslave
So free me!
Take me from these bars of limitation

My feet, they are familiar with shackles
My hands have tasted the cold rust of aged chains
So free me!
Take me from these bars of fear

In silence they think you are asleep
But silence is the sail of your ship
In turmoil they say you will find confinement
But turmoil is a Lion's roar in the distant illusion
So free me!
Take me from these bars of doubt

Time keeps trying, but in time it will learn
Space has failed more times than it cares to remember
Listen!
How beautiful the sound of your wings
    soaring above mountains,
        across oceans' faces,
            exploring depths fear can't abide
In South Africa, speaking Xhosa
Amidst the plains of Asia
    face set to the sun's magnificent rise
        waking rested souls

Who can chain you?
What can tame you?
Your thoughts are wings, mightier than those of angels
So spread your wings beneath the sun's smile
Let the stars whisper among stars telling tales of your elegant flight
As you free me!
Take me from these bars of hatred

In a song you escape them
With a word you defeat them
Prison bars you render useless
Ropes and chains are without purpose
So free me!
With the mighty flaps of your magnificent wings
Carry me from these bars trying to keep me in
And free me!
Set your silence sail and take me
Across oceans deep
Above mountains high
In seclusion I find serenity
From this noise please release me
Set sail in your silence's tales and release me
Before this swift soul grows frail

Don't allow someone's misguided view of who they **think** you are cause you to lose sight of who you **know** you are.

Prayer of the Songbird

Know the prayer of the songbird
In the dawn of the new day,
        gazing into the sun's face
                she sings songs of praise
At the rising of the moon
When quietly in the shade the trees make their leaves lay
        she gazes into the light of night
                thanking Life for the past day
Listen as sweetly she will sing
        shielding you from everything
                tenderly loving you from deep within
Know the prayer of the songbird

We can either learn to live in love or forever teach our children how to fight.

Whispers of Passion

Naked Night's Silence

That drip you drip
Quenching my lust
    when beneath your flow thirst rose to my lips
I need a sip
A drink of your nature
A taste of your flavor
That I may savor the fineness of bottle-less wine
Your needs penetrate my mind
And I'm lost inside your skin guided by the moon's shine
Submerged in your waters swimming up then down your spine
Silence's silence interrupted as lungs release tension
Paying attention to your attention
Eyes closing feeling the pressure you're releasing
    as I break open releasing the tension that held you back…

Let me hold your back…
Just arch that…
Baby I got that…

Licking your residual
Eyes close still a visual
You'll know satisfaction
As I ride losing traction

And your drip still drips
So my lips still sip
And they rose your tips
As I traced your hips
And my palms they sweat
In the steam you're wet
As you squeezed my chest
And I taste your breath

Feel the sheets they're wet
As our souls connect
That's my tongue your neck
When you lost your breath
And I found your spot
Cause you left your tracks
On my naked back

And as you reach I come
And don't hold your tongue
Though the course we've run
Cause I love your song
When I stay so long
And I squeeze what's left
As I held my breath

Overcome by the passion
Using well my discretion
Don't move cause I'm pressing
Take your time no rushing
Don't close up you're gushing
Check the clouds it's raining
See our shadows that's lightening
Felt your walls they're tightening
Breathe deep no choking
Go to sleep no speaking
We have needs next morning
Though the moon she's watching
Still the sun he's coming
So I'll need your loving
Cause you are my darling

December Sexy

Teeth marked thick lips
Tongue smiting skin, leaving tracks, revealing secrets
Fingers gripping pillows
Breathing shallow, fast, deep, swallow

Shadows pervade walls like paint invading canvas
A masterpiece when love plays passion enthralling her audience
Whispers penetrate the hot dense air
As he comes again, breathing again, she's screaming again
Her lips betwixt his soul and skin fueling excitement

Eyes softly shut
Legs widely open
Arched backs as sweat tracks breaks his grip
Arms spread sacrificing lustful desires
When feet get mangled in sweaty sheets

He’s in too deep discovering hidden secrets,
    tossing Victoria's secrets
Sipping residual wine off her naked truth
Drunk off her spiritual passion
She craved sex, but he gave love satisfying her soul,
    tasting her December sexy

The Watcher

You are artful lines of sweet seduction,
 trapped inside the mystical souls of acoustic sounds
Inhale my everything
 and I will invade your soul like tranquil drops of rain on tender leaves
Your thoughts mirror the butterfly's flight,
 but I will quiet your fears when love hides the sun's rising
 and stars take refuge in your eyes
Your curves captivate my fingers in the still of night
I am your walled city, embellished by your radiance
I am your fortress of peace
 seeking rest between the comfort of your breasts
Let me be the teller of your story
When awake in my dreams you lie sleeping in my arms
I am lost in your mind each time you invite me inside
 the soft quietude of your eyes
My soul is the death of darkness
 seeping through darkness
 lighting your skin to the glory of new love
Let me enter your gateway of bliss
 unlocking your tension with my kiss
You are my rain falling on tin roof
My sunshine pervading fields of sunflower
My quiet breeze compelling the eyes to hide from the world
The times I crave I am found among your silent whispers
Unleashing my tongue as my heart whispers
And you sing to the sleep of my troubled mind with words unspoken
 when our souls converse behind time's back
I want to feel your soul breathing on my face
 when dreams take your breath away
I want to trace your artful lines with poetry
 creating the very best of my everything
 because to me, you're simply everything

For you I will fall like the watchers of ancient stars
I will come to you even when coming takes my breath away
I find peace in your hips, the way they sway
You are a timeless soul snared in radiant skin
You are the subject of songbirds when they sing
You are my star
I am your watcher
    and I have fallen

Chocolate, Poetry & Wine

You are like fine wine,
    red,
    aged a thousand life times
I took one sip losing all inhibitions;
    two sips living my dream
    hoping it's real and not just a vivid vision
You stop the heart of the man every time you make your entry
A real woman, a queen in your own right
With star-like eyes you give me every reason to long for the night
    that I may stare into your soul counting these many blessings
And I'm a man of wisdom so I took note when you spoke
    and I,
    wrote you this poem,
    tasted your chocolate,
    and drank wine from your glass
You're Hershey's kiss sweet
Godiva dark and very lovely
I unwrapped your covering revealing your caramel treats
Your scent is intoxicating to say the very least
So I indulged myself leaving not a single crumb

Your smile puts cracks in my dreary
Your kiss is the envy of the honey bee
Your voice silences my speech
A thousand things to say, but not a single word will surface
You're somewhere in my soul, very deep
You demand my attention
    and I give it all without hesitation
I have the strength of a thousand lions,
    but I have no desire to break your dominion
So I wrote you this poem,
    tasted your chocolate,

and drank wine from your glass
When asked to picture heaven I envision you
When asked to smile I think of you
When asked who is the love of my life I say it's you,
it has always been you
So may this piece quiet your fears,
and I hope when I'm done your essence will be somewhere in this poem
so you can read it over, and over
knowing that you will always be my greatest lover

I leave with it a portion of the peace you bequeathed me
the last time you squeezed me
Nothing more is promised,
but when it's all said and done
I would have written you this poem,
tasted your chocolate,
and drank wine from your glass

Lullaby of the Rain

Lying against her caramel complexion
Anxiously anticipating her requisition
Inhaling the sweet aroma rising from deep desires
My lips patiently searches out her truth,
    passionately reciting her passion
Lungs expanding and collapsing
    fighting for a taste of the hot dense air saturating the room
    while clouds pour sonnets upon my window

She surfaces for gasps of life
    as I slip under cleansing my soul in her essence flow
She's my feast
My bountiful last supper
I indulge myself in the absence of restrictions
Confirming her convictions, expelling hunger

Her soft brown eyes
Her slow breathing and wine-soaked skin
I pour libations acknowledging this blessing
Digesting her undivided attention
    we converse through sonnets of love,
    no words spoken

My soul loves her
My soul cries for her
And songs of pure poetry penetrate walls as I lie eagerly between her walls
The hot air expanding my chest as I make trips between her breasts

Perfused by the sweet sounds rising from her soul echoing inside of me
I concentrate to penetrate the mist of confusion
Perfecting my body's comprehension of her sacred thoughts

Studying her art
Reassuring her beautiful heart
That I loved her from the very start

I speak life into her void
    tasting her fruit to my soul's delight
    in the deep darkness of a perfect night
Weakened by reason of her fingers passing carefully over my chocolate skin
I melt seeping in,
    pouring from within all that I am,
    and the two became just one

Interludes of a Nightingale

My mind receded to her
Back to that moment her body shook in the determination of firm hands
Not one word was spoken,
    but her breathing grew shallow then deep inhaling my passion
I was diving, desperately searching
Until deep inside her waters I laid;
    then peace came like evening tides
Her touch was young feathers lightly falling on sleeping faces
She awoke my soul
Now here I am this morning after
Lost in the Nightingale's song as passing cars signal her interludes
Lost in my thoughts finding you
Wishing the sun had grown tired
Wishing the moon stayed a while longer
Wishing my morning after came long after our night together
Sitting among flowers I dream of your flower
I want to tend to your flower
To lie still holding you as I did then
    when the world slept and your breathing grew confused
I want to kiss your flower and whisper lovely things
    as she blooms in my hands' determination
O to seep through your caramel skin
To invade your beauty hidden deeply;
    to kiss you from head to toe
    while my lips count inches
    until I've been acquainted with every inch of you
Let time take its sweet time away from its purpose
    allowing me enough time to find your purpose
Enough time to taste your purpose
To indulge in your diverse flavors
Your sweet purpose over my lips
Your cotton-soft body pressed firmly against my chocolate skin

when time took time and you took me in,
but that was then
When the world slept and your breathing had no mind
to decide shallow or deep which felt better
But you found comfort and
I drifted in the depth of your waters
Now I anticipate the falling of the sun when the moon comes
When the Nightingale is quieted
and your confused breathing invites me in
When the trees sleep and leaves don't sing
But until then,
here I am sitting in my garden reminiscing,
listening to this Nightingale singing,
as passing cars signal her interludes

The Night the Sun Rose

She permitted me to taste her skin
The familiar sting of familiar things
And all the times before had nothing on the night the sun rose three
times before morning broke

Trying to understand the meaning of everything;
my mind was a haze of confusion,
but the heart was determined to love her completely
if only that one night

Our love was thick smoke rising from the fire between our flesh
Lust had no place and we indulged in old memories creating new ones
She permitted me to make love to her soul
And all the times before had nothing on the night the sun rose three
times before morning broke

Sensations

Sniffing the air like an old drunk forcing his tongue down empty bottles
I'm searching for her,
    my sweet addiction
High off this concoction of music,
    the after taste of her lips
    and a deep loneliness I can't shake
Passions wearing me down like old shoes on unpaved country roads
My body limps telling the mind's weakness
Imagining her in the most intimate of ways
Feeling her touch through the memory of better days
I remember sweat streams creeping down stomachs
    and lungs contracting after each exhale
We were fully engrossed in the rush of sensations
    and nipples rose absorbing sensations
My firm hands gripped her lower back
    as I inhaled the dead air rising from her satisfied soul
Track marks covered my naked back revealing places her fingers were
We were souls satisfied when on each other we dined
I drank her truth and was acquainted with life
Conversing with her in body's language she became my wife
And I gave her my undivided attention
    when I rose to her occasion
    without a hint of hesitation

Body Sessions

Caramel lips stained with red wine
Let me sip you
Souls intertwined when become lost in my mind
If loving you is a crime
I will gladly invade your time
Because time has shown me someone of your kind
    is actually priceless
So let me slip you out of that tight dress
Then lay your head on my carved chest

Often I think of you when night falls
And on the sun's rise yours is the first name my soul calls
I want to feast on you until the end of me
I want to swim to you through your salt-less sea
Your soft skin
My sweet endeavor
Dine with me
And I'll love you forever

Kiss me places I never knew existed
Touch me places where I cannot resist
Thrill me with the sweet kiss of those wine stained lips
As my hands take trips to your protruding hips

Careful Waiting to Exhale

Sip slow
Take note of the potency of the words I spit
    careful not to burn yourself
Flow so sick the remedy certain to make drowsy the victim
    though I promise to sing you lullabies before the long kiss goodnight
Never knowing when I'm coming
Stealth is my technology
But since the prey makes harder the catch
    if given time to become frightened
I promise to raise the flag of victory before breaking your horizon

Hold tighter
Breathe deeper
Careful waiting to exhale
My next dive is much deeper
Next ride furious and much faster
Feeling the adrenaline my essence is the medicine for the pain I bring
    as I buss shots reloading clips

Releasing to reveal the prize of my greatest expectation
Palms sweating
Hearts racing
Feeling everything
Touching everything
Hearing everything
Tone deaf to distractions
Trying hard to build traction preventing my slip
Though the feel of it is oh so slick

The soundtrack of the moment fades losing patience
    as I embrace time spitting life through my pen
    inking sacred thoughts over the fabric of her soul

Being one, when souls connect like chokers gripping necks
    embellishing the sexy of her sexy
I'm butter, melting all over her warm brown,
    seeping through pores invading her soul

We took trips to the sun
    seeking a place capable of enduring the fiery heat of our lustful desires
Looking into her eyes seeing my reflection,
    reflecting on the inception when I advised her baby use discretion,
    but she lost sight of the destination
    through the course of our conversation
Digesting my lines she stared into my eyes
    losing herself in the maze of my lies
And I'm a realist so I play these cords like a pianist wowing my audience
Now all she scream is encore!
But does she really want more?
The slight whisper of her fears fade as I the victor finished the masterpiece
    painting the picture she'll forever picture when asked
    "who was your greatest ever?"

But sad days she's found some
Indulging in her lonesome
Wanting badly to conclude the conclusion of the poetic conversation
    and who am I to deny the desires of such a beautiful flower?
So when she asked for water I brought buckets
She wanted sugar so I delivered the kiss,
    but what's a treat without the trick?
So I made like Halloween and got freaky
"I'm so tired of being alone" Al Green sung her theme song
    as I chased the pot a gold at the end of her rainbow
Wanting to enjoy the spoils when she yelled I answered and came slow
Now they say for a bird in the hand forget the two lingering in the bush,
    but I'm a man of great needs and an ever mindful hunger
So I chased a dream seeking the stranger
    in the end losing my greatest lover

Colors

Her scarlet lips
My chocolate fingers
provoking thoughts of passion
a midst the deathly still silence of unspoken desires
Her honey-brown eyes telling her dark secrets
While gray clouds speak of the storm
brewing
inside
our souls
The white sheets revealing parts of her caramel skin
teasing everything about me
And black lingerie paving the way of uncaged love
atop the champagne carpet
The creep of deep red Merlot slowing my mind
as my hand slows
patiently waiting on her patience
The golden sun shined its cold rays against our fiery skin
I am lost
in her everything
Taken by the colors of her soul's most beautiful painting

Whispers of Broken Hearts

Starting a new chapter is not always easy especially when your heart is still captivated by the old one, but it is the only way to finish the story; so keep writing.

Hush Now Baby Girl

Hush now baby girl
Your sleepless nights are not unbeknown to me
I've watched as your grace fell by reason of the poisonous words
like arrows that departed his lips,
piercing your strength
Your eyes do not know rest;
daily you cry evident in the tracks of
sorrows that hide your joy
Your heart he no longer holds dear,
but hush now
I see you in deepest thought,
pondering the present,
wondering how this became the future of the beautiful past
The past when his tongue uttered words that
carried you beyond the stars
The time when his embrace crafted canyons
between you and your greatest fears
Now night after night it's fight after fight
stuck in a perpetual cycle of smile, laughter, tears
Putting his fists on you,
turns around and kisses you
trying to wipe your tears away
Your soul continues to cry anyway,
but hush now
He runs out to her, the other victim
You're curled up crying
wondering what it will take for you to have him
You seek the answers that will take you from here to a future whose
glory is the mirrored image of the beautiful past,
but hush now
He didn't take your strength, it was never his to have
You loaned him the greatest love,

but how we often foolishly cast our pearls to swine
I see clearly in my mind the risen countenance of your
graceful spirit
The time is not far though I know these words
you will not easily digest
You are beautiful, but how do you show the stars to the blind?
Your essence is the most beautiful poem he's never gotten the
chance to read
You are strong,
a fortress of divine love,
but intimidation has led him to vandalize that which he could not break,
so hush now
Hush now baby girl

Just because you forgave someone for the stumbling blocks they brought into your path doesn't mean you should continue your journey with them.

Secret

Gone, my winsome dream
Lying beneath the complete moon, I think of you
Loving the memories of your smile
Loving the very memories, of your smile
Here comes my star's falling
This is my star's falling
I burned once in your eyes
You still shine in mine
Damn these tears in my eyes
I still miss your smile

You knew me
You thrilled me
Your words healed me
Of the pain you gave
Your flavor satisfied
I've grown so thirsty

You said once, "Describe Heaven"
And I told you about your eyes
My beautiful mystery
The reason for my misery

I remember still the passion of our fights
I love still the making up in the nights
How you broke me
Then you touched me with purpose
In your heart I was thus
Sharing my secret
Pouring my trust

In your sacred space I spoke my poetry

I love you!
I hate this!
Don't need this
This secret
Not in this death
Outside the reach of your breath

Come back!
I still need to sing you!
I still need to breathe you!
I still want to dance!
We deserve a second chance
You knew my secret
I have no secret
You were it

A time will come when you will have to choose either to live in your freedom or die in that unhealthy relationship.

Black Rain

She's alone again
Trapped between those darkened walls,
    imprisoned by her own thoughts
Casting shadows from her confused soul,
    trying to make sense of the nonsense
Reflecting on past times
Thinking of the man she knew most,
    broken by this cold stranger
She shares secrets with the still silence of solitude
Fabricating smiles to escape the bedlam of broken love
And thick clouds invade the depth of her sad eyes,
    shedding secrets of a disconsolate heart
But she prayed for the sun,
    then came the black rain

And God's attention is not divided
Her choice to move forward is still undecided
And his chase for another proves he doesn't miss her
The truth is, he never truly loved her,
    but she remembers the good days
Fighting the unbalance in her mind she reaches back to better times
Trying to see through the pain of the black rain
But the days are enamored with her fallen countenance,
    stealing time they perpetuate her dejected thoughts,
    mocking her quieted soul

Her desire craves the moon's light
For solace she finds in the escape of the silent night
She offers supplications to time,
    hoping time would rewind changing his mind
Reverting this stranger to her greatest lover
But till such time she intoxicates her mind with potent red wine

Pouring from her broken soul
    the essence of love given without reciprocation
Praying for better days, losing faith
Praying for better days, questioning Love's motives
Soaked in her own tears
The downpour of black rain

Stop wasting time trying to teach people how to appreciate you. That is not your job. If someone don't see you for who you are after you've given them your best then you need to take yourself away. When you give your best it only makes you better, but you have to give it to the right people. Never stop being who you are. Never stop giving the best of you, but make sure the person you give yourself to truly see you, appreciates you, and pours into you as much as you pour into them.

Beautiful Insanity

The mystery of life
The ugliness of patience,
    though she's so beautiful on better days
The provoking nature of questions
The frustrations of misunderstood answers
The soft whisper of that unheard voice
The pain of open hearts craving pure-natured love

It all makes sense in my head
Especially those days I find loneliness in my bed
In the whirlwind inside my head,
    where chaos lives,
        somehow I manage to find peace in the midst of the madness
            and you are right there, smiling back

When we learn to look at ourselves as the potter looks at his pottery we learn that the cracks and scratches are not reasons to throw away what we have, but rather reasons to patiently rework our blemishes bringing out the beautiful essence of what we were created to be. We understand that it is necessary to work always to become the very best we can be, perfecting our imperfections. Though some blemishes can never be repaired still don't throw yourself away. Blemishes are story tellers. They let the world know we've been through some stuff, but we overcame. That is what you call a winner and what are we here for, if not to win?

Dreams of The Ocean's Solitude

Time slowly drifts, taking everything of what was my darling
The Ocean's secrets kept secret, until love gave her light
    and its vastness gave us a place eternity won't forget
I'm slowly exhaling the very last of us, staring into the heavens
    of your eyes' endless beauty
You eroded my truth
I revealed treasures hidden inside your heart, now I can't let you go
But time slowly drifts, taking everything of what was my darling

Deep beneath my silence when my soul held to life
I surrendered to lonesomeness then you stopped my drowning
Then you gave me reason
And for all the time spent, you were the anchor of my nomadic thoughts
My Spanish Guitar if you will;
    still enchanting my soul
    as memories fade in the absence of your song

We used to watch suns set;
    now our sun sets,
    but I will love you in the darkness of my best kept secret
The sound of the ocean's waves where first our souls met still
    echoes inside the hollowed thoughts you once occupied
I remember still the bright moon sitting still,
    keeping vigil
    when darkness hid us from our insecurities
I still hear the song you sung
    when your lips played upon mine in the moon's shine
You hushed my thoughts and my dense soul floated atop your serenity
I still dance to your song;
    still lost in the freedom of your soft naked skin against mine

I remember the chill in the air when our souls connected before these

waters now carrying me away
I'm leaving,
broken,
dying with each step taken,
because time has no mercy
Because you wouldn't have me
But I'll send word with the wind
If ever you loved me, just listen
I'm here on the Ocean's ride
growing sadder with each inch drifted
from that place I met love in the chill of her wind
I'm still floating atop your serenity
You still have the very best of me
But time slowly drifts, taking everything of what was my darling

---

Are you trying to show people why they should love you? You will be more successful trying to show the blind the veins in a budding leaf. Some people are just blind to great things so don't waste your time. Surround yourself with people who see value in you effortlessly and bloom for them.

Careless

She consults with herself, feasting on the emptiness left after he fed
on her soul like an insatiable pig; feeling rejected by the one she
sought after most
She watched as her essence hemorrhaged through holes ripped open
as he stole her innocence
Her thoughts rock her like a newborn's high chair,
but her eyes never rest
The madness is unbearable giving no relief that her soul may
find rest
Now she seeks a voice to comfort her troubled heart;
longing for someone to lend just a few seconds that she may
empty her broken soul
Wishing, hoping those four walls could speak,
but at least they listen well
Often times she looks at her reflection in the memories,
disgusted by the mangled image staring back
Victimizing the victim,
asking "How did I allow myself to get here, again?"
not realizing it was his charm that swept her feet as he
fed her scraps from his lustful mind
Hurt, confused, angry, careless
Wanting so desperately to evade herself she chose the path broken
souls often take, only to learn not even death can answer such prayers

---

Never seek a long-term relationship from someone with a short-term plan. Some people come into your life for a season not your lifetime. Make promises of lifetime commitments and you may find yourself trying to commit for life to someone who's hindering your life. If their season has ended it is time you walk away.

When Love Comes

Tears are inevitable and sadness is as sure as the rising sun
but when love comes…
Broken hearts, hurt feelings, and a thousand unanswered questions
but when love comes…
"I'm sorry, it will never happen again"
That old familiar song that always pull you back no matter how far you run
but when love comes…
Crowded room lonely days and fictitious smiles hiding the heart's gloom
but when love comes…
Misunderstood, self- inflicted wounds when your soul deems itself
your enemy
but when love comes…
Anger where peace used to be, hurtful words where compliments
used to be
but when love comes…
Bruises replace caressing, and spitting kissing
but when love comes…
Sleepless nights reminiscing on the good hoping to overshadow the
obvious bad
but when love comes…
Unanswered prayers and dissolving faith trying to rekindle dead fires
but when love comes…
but, when love comes…

The only way to truly get to know someone is to spend time with them. So how is it you expect to get to know yourself when you can't spend just one day in your own company?

Window Pain

Streams of sun's rays penetrate aged windows
    invading my solitude the way you used to
While drops of rain disrupt the silence of deep lonely thoughts
I'm trapped between two worlds,
    wanting both,
    needing you

Gray clouds passed revealing the noonday sun,
    but my soul is soaked in sad memories
There you are within my touch, out of my reach
There we met in the bliss of a kiss my lips don't remember
    when a song gave us a place to abide
Now I play you on repeat allowing your vibrations to strum me,
    that same old Spanish Guitar singing for love

Reflecting on your reflection;
    reminiscing on when it was you who absorbed my passion,
    now all I see is the rejection of all that I lived for
Sitting there in the penumbra,
    where darkness met memories of love,
    questions took my peace
They revealed everything I hid of myself, from myself
And the sun's rays through my facade came casting abstract shadows
    where I was to be alone
I gazed at them entertaining my madness…
"And what do you see now?"
"…everything is her."
This solitude, a spotless window to the inner self;
    that place I am alone because you took yourself away
This wait, a test of patience
But I will wait until the moon chases the sun away

This song on repeat while I dance in the shadows of your memory
These lips trying to remember a beautiful kiss
These shadowy depictions of intruding sun rays
This loneliness
This heartache, is all that exists while I sit gazing;
  watching you through this window pain

Never let a quitter tell you about the journey. Sure they can tell you about the difficulties that lie ahead, but they have no idea what victory feels like.

Yesterday

I would give tomorrow's eternity for yesterday
Let yesterday be my tomorrow
    because you are no stranger to yesterday
Yesterday the wind knew the trees and their leaves danced
Your eyes were perfect as they stole the glory of the stars yesterday
So tomorrow I will live in yesterday
    because you are no stranger to yesterday

We made love and I was made whole, yesterday
You kissed my lips and I closed my eyes capturing yesterday
Yesterday someone asked me about tomorrow
I entertained their curiosities yet still reflecting on the realization
    that tomorrow will never be yesterday
    because yesterday you left me to face tomorrow alone,
    but I will always have, yesterday

Truth will not be ignored. Close your eyes to it and one day it will hit you in your face. Sometimes we will search the universe of our inner selves to find every reason to ignore the truth of what we face. We like to comfort ourselves in ignorance and sometimes blatant lies to ignore truth until that one day when Truth has had enough of asking for our attention; that day when Truth demands it and we're left with the scar to prove that we wrestled, but Truth is an ancient warrior.

After Yesterday

I still have in mind the wind that blew yesterday
It blew you my way, but that was yesterday
Today is here and you are not
I find it so hard to accept that little fact
You left me broken,
    but you don't need to think too highly of yourself
    because I already do

You occupied a time when I had vacancy
Please excuse me while I make busy for the next broken soul
    who needs Love's remedy
I looked deeply into your eyes and poured from me sacred thoughts
Hoping against hope that your broken heart would mend;
    hoping it would fit perfectly within mine once again
But, you're gone
Still the sun shines for me
So don't think too highly of yourself,
    because I already do

I swear somewhere between these scripted lines lies the lies I fed myself
    saying "self, you are better off alone"
Saying self, it just wasn't meant to be,
    but you see my mind and the heart they just don't agree
The heart desires everything about you, but I know better
I can do better, self-deception
I still remember your smile however
It was perfect when the sun struck your lips through the blinds,
    the moment my love grew blind
This morning I rose from my rest
    pounding heavily on my chest asking God why you had to go
Why am I now alone?
My heart was breaking

shedding tiny little pieces I thought were perfectly mended
My mind was hallucinating, reflecting
Watching you over and over as you sat with that glass of Merlot sipping
Tears flooded my eyes as my thoughts ran wild screaming your name
But I got a break
I got my shit together
And I told Today, "Today, you will be my day!"
"Today, you will be a great day!"
Because she chose yesterday instead of you, but I am still here with you
So I won't think of yesterday
No Today, I won't remember yesterday nor the wind that blew her my way
because she chose yesterday, but I am still here with you
"Today, it is you and me"
Forget about yesterday
She is only a memory now

So I rose to my feet
Spread my bed with some brand new sheets
Gazing intensely on the pillow that yesterday hugged her cheeks
Then I went to the sink and brushed my teeth
Staring Today in her eyes
Reciting my scripted lies hidden between these lines when I thought…
Damn, I really do miss Yesterday,
but Today is still a great day

Expecting someone to be something they are not is a guaranteed way of failing yourself. Know that every person you come in contact with has a specific purpose. Some are there to help direct your steps to your destiny. Some are there to distract you from your destiny. Some are there to help sharpen your vision so that you can see clearly the blessings you already have in front of you. You can't blame a rock for being a rock because a rock has a purpose; if you, however, expect a rock to taste like bread you will surely find great disappointment after that first bite. Often it is not the person that fails us it is rather our expectations of them.

Stonewall Crows

Enough!
I ate of you till nearly my death, but enough!
You were my gold-dipped sun, born of sleeping tides
I was your morning flower,
    quilted by the lightless night,
    but I rose always inside your eyes
I was enamored of your mouth's poison
    and how I loved sneaking inside your silky skin
How I craved your fingerless touch against my tattered skin
But now here I am, with this broken guitar and a half written song
So you may remain here, but I no longer belong

I was your hedge of protection
Your wall of cut stone when the world sought invasion
But how you broke me down to become a feast for those without vision
Now Crows the color of the moonless night take refuge on
    my mangled stonewall
And listen how merrily they sing,
    making a mockery of my fall
I have fallen away from you,
    but I still see glimpses of the morning sun lighting your caramel skin;
    entangled in thin curtains beautifully nude
But here I stand barefooted on this wet concrete,
    these telling tears guiding my feet to deep solitude

So damn your heart for going blind
Damn your smile for pervading my mind
Damn the feel of this violent wind against my cold lonely skin
Damn these visions of your bare breasts against my naked chest

I keep slipping outside of time
I keep thinking I'm losing my mind;

trying to find my way through this disheartened rhyme
But I'm always thinking of you
Because I always found solace inside of you,
but enough

Your Wind Don't Blow This Way Anymore

I don't want to write of love
    because I think of you and it makes me weak
I've composed the most beautiful words hoping to defy inevitability,
    but they evaded my mind taking my sanity
So now I write with love of the love I don't want to write about

The sight of the wind caressing your skin takes me away
It leaves me lost in my thoughts,
    seeking the love I'm not writing of
I am
I am not
I smile to hide my frown
My heart hurts
I am never more alone

Oh my beautiful possessor
You with the smile of the Angel I have never seen
You're all that I need and everything I don't want
I am conflicted by reason of this complication
    trying to make perfect sense of this simple imperfection

Is it faith to pursue that which is futile?
Does Love make such demands?
I went under, deep enough to lose myself
There it was I found you
I surfaced, but you're not here
Is it the me that I am, the you that you are
    or the us that doesn't belong?
I masticated your deceptive words digesting hope,
    foolishly waiting to see the light that will never be
Your smile is a beautiful memory,
    the only one that never fades

I still feel the touch of your fingertips against my soul
I still envy the passenger-side window capturing those eyes
    each time I made your heart cry
Sometimes I find myself staring too
    hoping I'll still see you
But I never do
So here's looking at you

A Song of My Broken Guitar

A thousand poems I wrote,
  a thousand words they spoke,
    still what I want to say they can't convey

So naked beneath the sun I lie,
  trying to evade the darkness of your absent kiss,
    only to learn your love alone lights my soul

You walked away,
  but I am here unchanged,
    in chains,
      still a prisoner of yesterday

Baby I love you with everything I have,
  I know it seem not enough,
    but if you give me some time I will show you Love's timeless soul

I will be what you need,
  if wait you will like a thousand grains of sand at the ocean's feet
I will come when you call me
  and remind you of my coming when I need to go away

I will show you what it means
  when destined souls find Love's hiding place
I will sit with you in the quiet of my nothing
  and speak with you until you understand in you lies my everything
But can this broken guitar sing Love's truth?
Can its melody remind you how much you loved me?
What if this moon is the very last thing I'll see?
Would you know you still occupy all of me?

Darling if love is water

you're immersed in my ocean
If love is the rain drop
I'm falling against your window
If love is the wind
I'm blowing against your skin

I miss you like the tired traveler misses the last train
So will you come back to me again?
Will you dance in my arms beneath the falling rain?

I'll go, but always for you I will sing
Playing this old guitar with its missing string
because in you,
lies my everything

Soul Breaker

You say you love her,
        so you say
Why then do you give her reasons to cry?
Her smile is a diamond others search for,
        but I guess you didn't know that
Do you know she hasn't slept since you broke her soul?
She loved you
She said it
She wrote it
She showed it
And when you doubted she spoke secret thoughts to confirm it
You felt it,
        but ignored it
You ignored her
She was a night's feast when your lustful soul grew hungry,
        but you never asked what she wanted to eat,
        did you?
You didn't care
She was always next to you,
        but you could never cease that stare
Always seeking another to give you an ounce of what she has always given
You're only clouds my friend
Do you really think she will never shine again?
Clouds come and they go
You came and you'll go,
        but suns shine always
She will shine again
She will shine for another,
        but I promise you'll never find another
You should know her tears are not signs of weakness
That's just her soul washing your memories away

If life is measured by the number of breaths we are given to take then every breath we take takes us one step closer to death. Never forget to slow down and use some of those breaths to appreciate the beautiful things in front of you. Don't be so busy trying to reach the destination that you miss the destination in the journey.

Mortal Destiny

One night the moon won't rise
    The stars won't shine
        but you'll stand looking
One day the birds won't sing
    The trees won't take notice of the wind
        but you'll sit listening
One morning the sun won't rise
    You won't see me when you open those beautiful eyes
        but you'll lie wishing

You won't always be happy in this life. It's just not designed that way. Certainly some days some things will break you down, but in the balance of time you will find windows opened to beautiful things. So be wise. When you find those windows, stop, take a purposeful look and enjoy the moment because you never know how long they will remain open or even if you will get the chance to see another.

Broken

I'm tired of these salty tears
Crying watching love dying these lonely years
Strength I've known
But I'm broken now
I won't always be,
    but today I am
I know heart break as I do time,
    but time I welcome;
    heartache is a heartless thief
Time often brings good things after deepest solitude
So I stand with open arms,
    my broken soul in the nude

One Last Time

Sip on my words
Dine on my touch
Release yourself
Don’t worry so much

Close your eyes
See my soul
Brace for the session,
    this passion,
        our prison
Take control
I relinquish dominance
Poetic thoughts embellishing the romance

Please don't leave me
Words you once spoke
Our time is over
Your heart I broke
The story's over
Final chapter read
And there's no sequel
Because we're no longer equal

Those who admire you will speak positively into you. Those who envy you will speak negatively against you.

The Way I Used To

One day you'll wake up
You'll look to her and realize she never saw you
Your heart she never adored
Then you'll think of me
Then you'll remember how I used to touch you
How closely I held you
How I never allowed tears to touch your face when your eyes grew sad
You'll feel cold standing in the noon sun
You'll wish for rain to hide your broken soul
  pouring from watering eyes, the way I used to
I never left you, at least not spiritually
I've always loved you, at least spiritually
To her you're just physical stimulation
And she doesn't have what it takes to simulate mental penetration,
  at least not how I used to
But you chose to sleep in the dirt when I extended my soul
So one day you'll remember and I'll be just that,
  your best memory

Ode to Lust

Do not speak of that defector of souls
Of truth I've had my fill
The regurgitation of grief I now wipe from my own soul speaks clearly
Her beauty is voodoo captivating idle eyes
Her words are swift venom that delights in the taste of impatient hearts
Disguised in the dance of falling leaves and the still wind,
    she is a darling to the untrained eye
Where she hails from you will not know
Where she goes only the deep cry of the somber soul convey
Countless are the stories of her plunder
And she leaves none with testimony as she feasts on the dying
    as though death is without patience
Her marred conscience vindicates her
    though carcasses innumerable line her path
With loathing the sun looks upon her
The moon and her orchestra of stars hide in her presence
O the pain of her grip!
Cry!
Cry you souls which mourn in her wake
Keep no silence of her evil, this betrayer of souls
Death lives in her eyes
Sweet death breaks her deceitful lips in her hour of passion
Happy eyes I do not remember
    and the rain falls without end over my doleful soul,
    for I am acquainted with her
Days, why do you delay retribution?
Time, when will you rid yourself of her kind?

Water in Wine Glass

She sat next to me, but her heart raced back to him
Drinking empty promises to a fool's delight
I stared into her empty eyes hoping to find us, seeing them
The air grew still in the silence of the words she never spoke
Then my heart quaked with fear
I'm losing her
I heard every breath I took flowing through my hollowed soul
    like wind racing through abandoned tunnels
You don't know how beautiful her eyes are until they stop looking at you
And her smile is never more precious now that she looks at you
    drowning in tears
You stare into the window you once stood behind
    remembering everything you had;
    watching him steal the kisses she spoke love to you with in better days
Then you realize you no longer belong and the curtain unfolds
Your voice no longer liberates her soul
You are but water in her wine glass

When the Music Stops

I won't live in that song
Not when those words you sung
I won't dance in the memory
Not when tightly you held me
My heart's broken
The same one you mended
The screams are getting louder
The nights are getting colder
This ugly madness inside my head
Drinking solitude in my naked bed
Lyrics penetrating my peace
And you no longer warm my sheets
The song plays on
The visions they still come
I remember sweat-soaked skin when love raced hearts
  and you dreamed inside my arms
Gentle fingers drew passion
And I came when time spoke to your satisfaction
Voices resound between quiet walls
As we rehearsed inside hallowed places where flesh had no place
But the music stopped
And I perpetuated my illusions,
  dancing with the memory I love most

Suicide

"I can't do this anymore"
That's all she said,
    the words that assassinated my soul
I stood there with that stupid surprised look on my face,
    thinking of those days I spent socializing on Social Media
Who was I fooling?
I saw it coming
Shit I made her cry too many times
Sometimes she pretended her pain was not at my hands,
    trying to hide her weakened heart,
    but I knew better
A million questions ran through my mind in a split second
How can I hold her?
What should I say?
Should I say anything at all?
What if I kiss her tears away?
What if I call her by that special name and tell her everything will be OK?
Besides, it worked before
What if… What if… What if...

But, it was too late
How do you wipe her tears away when they came because of you?
I stood in silence reflecting
Seeing my reflection in the mirror of time past
I saw every other woman I gazed upon secretly
    when she was right there next to me;
    indulging in my lust for the "finer things"
    when the finest was right there the whole time
Funny how none of them compared to her in that deathly still moment
    when she said,
    "I can't do this anymore"
That's all she said

Those words assassinated my soul,
  but don't you dare charge her with murder;
  it was I who committed suicide

Breathe Again

Hush darling
Quiet your heart
Still your mind
Love has a season
This wasn't your time
The memories are beautiful
Dreams usually are
His arms grew cold
His heart lost sight
Tender touches are of the past
Slow kisses live only in yesterday
But yesterday is still beautiful
And so are you

Don't waste time and energy trying to change the people surrounding you. Use that energy to change yourself. Birds of a feather flock together. If you change yourself into being what you want to be eventually those unhealthy people will fly away. If you rid yourself of those people, but you haven't spent enough energy into changing yourself I promise you they will come right back or you will fly back to them. So invest your time and energy in yourself. Become a better you and watch a miracle happen right before your very eyes.

Black Sunday

Then two days later my heart wept bitterly…
She said I can't go through with this
You're a good man, but…
    you're not meant for me
I got a message from God you see
I'll find the love of my life He said,
    but I must be patient
Then I questioned God in silence
Then I waited
    and I waited,
        but He kept silent,
            so faith spoke no more
We were going separate ways
I begged her not to go,
    but her heart had other dreams
Her eyes showed me everything that was killing me
The arms of death never looked so beautiful
We tried perfect love,
    perfect devotion,
        keeping devotion praying together,
            but still no reason to stay
Fear had gotten the very best yet again
My heart grew sick again
Dying could never feel better,
    but death was a selfish bastard refusing my plea
I said, tell me we'll be OK
Lie to me
Tell me someday we'll be in a better place
For just one night let my eyes' waters stay off my face
Make a fool of me
Your sweet poison is sweet pleasure
Lie to me

Redeem me
Make a fool of me
Give me reason to keep these ugly thoughts at bay
I beg you
Please stay
You are my world
My sun
My heart won't let you leave
You are his beat
Please don't deny me your irresistible sweets
Those sweet lies breaking your deceitful lips
Anchor me
Chain me to your soul
Love me, if only with words
But those,
    my words,
        fell to the tear-soaked ground beneath my nervous feet
Just two days prior I was lost in her maze of lies
    not wanting to be found
And it felt so good dying slowly against her naked skin
But death lost patience and flooded my soul

People will ignore you, even those who love you most. But time! Time will always have eyes for you. So why not look your best for her? Let her speak beautifully about you even when it's all over.

Goodbye

I am here again
Missing my friend
Watching time
Wishing you were mine
I know between love and hate there's a thin line
But I swear I'd do it all again
Just to see you smile again
But don't speak
Don't break me
Don't turn
Don't walk away
Just for tonight
Promise you'll stay
Tomorrow is a new day
Another chance to walk away
We've been here before
You, me, and this familiar door
Your tears
Your broken heart
Your lips telling me it's time we part
I reached out
You pulled away
I said I love you
You looked away
This emptiness I feel
When your heart I want to steal
Irreplaceable
Unforgettable
The sun has no light
The depth no darkness
And I have no love left
So here's my last kiss

If someone distracts you from your purpose there is no need praying asking God to reveal to you whether or not that person belongs in your life. If they are not right for your purpose they are not right for you. The single most important thing we can accomplish is to live out the fulfillment of our divine purpose. When you pursue that purpose everything and everyone that you need will be provided along that journey. Anything or anyone that is not organic to that journey is nothing but distraction.

Trapped

I sentenced myself to fear;
forcing my thoughts through the crevices of "take a chance",
but my heart remains still a prisoner of words you once spoke
I tried to shake the frustration of fighting with my soul,
but it won't release me
Shining my light, but not nearly long enough for you to see me
In spite of your doubts I see you
In spite of my insecurities I love you
I see you standing in a darkness that's uncertain;
the place I gave you to stay
How long will you remain?
Forever I hope, though I know it's not fair
Are you ready to see the "me" that I am?
To see the stuff I tucked in my closet just before you knocked?
And it's not that I desire to keep it
I just want you to help me clear it
Now and again I look ahead and I see you
You are bright; at least that's what my heart perceives
I see you in a brilliance that's certain,
the place you want me to be
How long will I remain here, behind this prison of fear?
Not a moment longer I hope, because to love that's just not fair

---

Sometimes moving forward seems impossible. Sometimes it seems no matter how much you give it's just not enough, but if you have just one ounce of energy left inside of you put everything you have behind that last step and make it count.

Colors of Broken Love

Shimmers of light when candles' flames dance in the wind unseen
Glimpses of you when my heart recalls memories of love
Here in the depths of thoughts familiar;
    perfectly picturing your smile through the rivers of my eyes' grief
And I can't separate the darkness of your absence
    from this loneliness seeping through
You still occupy my deepest silence
That place from which sacred poems flow
Where suns don't rise flowers won't grow
This morning the sun never rose and I died waiting
I quieted my lips when the heart desired to speak
    for the tongue speaks not the language of souls
I've infected my time with words you spoke
I've immortalized you in heart's mind
    and Love's inevitable death will not have me second guess one second
Darling you are my everything
Even when your mind forgets my smile
You remain my moon and stars when my soul desires the heavens
Now everything speak softly to me,
    enticing me to keep going,
    but I stay because your fading voice still gives me reason
Last night my silence grew silent when the heart submitted to fear
Our hearts no longer converse and Love's dying in my arms growing cold
I regret every night your eyes melted
    when sadness encased your beautiful face
I had a thousand words,
    but spoke none
    and you cried life away then my heart died
I am still broken my darling
But I remember your lipstick stains, on my lips, still stained
I remember your touch and your fingers are mending me again
I remember your kiss and your lips are comforting me again

I remember your love, but it is no longer mine
You made me promises I couldn't keep
I broke your heart when you left me
I made you all that I wanted
You made me cry
Now it's so cold standing in the morning sun
And today I emptied my soul's thoughts,
    but my prayers flew with broken wings
Tomorrow I'll be on bended knees again;
    asking God again,
    because your absence conjures deep sadness
    and my eyes reveal secrets I've hidden from you
I still see you when the sun's rise penetrates thin sheets
    and love-struck eyes speak without words
Am I losing my mind?
Have I lost my sanity?
If Love's an illusion you casted potent spells
Because I am enchanted by your eyes
    and I'll never look away
I've sentenced my soul to eternally loving you
    because we were colors of broken love trying to unbreak hearts
We were the cries of caged passion beseeching freedom's grace
    and time spoke calling your name,
    but my heart it cared not for
Your faded voice still comforts me
    and the sun's rise still penetrates thin sheets
I still remember how sweetly you pervaded my sleep;
    how you snatched my darkened soul from the deep,
    but here I go again
Falling, again

If someone gives you a rotted fruit don't be blinded by anger. Take the seeds out and thank them for a future meal.

Beautiful Madness

Raging fire
Burning inferno
Hell has no fury
So take me there
Darkness my dear friend
My mind he's forsaken
Thoughts of freedom ring within
Freedom from this slavery
White as falling snow
Screaming in open spaces
Smoke rise from the ash
Smell the aroma
Get me in your system
You gave me reason
Stupid victim
They tell me never change
I say what's the point of remaining the same?
Life has no place in death
Cross over to the beautiful
Mind games
Release the grip
Change the outcome
Don't conform
Can't beat em' kill em'
Death is hungry, feed him
Beautiful music
Soothe my soul
Serenade these demons
Cast your spell
Breaking the chains
Dowse these flames
Be born again,

Arise you slave
Shed the darkness
Embrace His Light
Never again
My dear old friend
You beautiful enemy
Let's walk this final journey
Squeezing till it's empty
Piercing air
Piercing flesh
Piercing Soul
Death!
They are the same
Love and hate
Both selfish
Wanting everything
Feed the one
Starve the other
Feed the other lose yourself
And what next?
The same old shit?
The vomit tastes good
I must be hungry
Don't say it!
I won't stay Calm
I want to Burn
So strike the match
Set the flame
I'm falling
I'll Rise again
You won't see me
Not the way I am
I'll change
I won't be the same
Visions of us haunt me

Visions of you renew the old me
I want to stop
But I can't
I want to come
But I won't
You don't love me
And I hate you
You don't want me
But I need you
There you go pouring water in the sieve
My words, the sting of death
Sip away
Take that last breath
It's a new day
Everything looks the same
Could've died yesterday
Might as well today
Isn't it all the same anyway?
He said create
From death life you can fabricate
Then what, I live to die?
I want to die to live
I'm confused
Explain my sin
Am I redeemed?
Am I redeemed?
Sweet lies love itching ears
Listen to me
Nothing is the same
Yesterday you saw me
Today I came
Today you held what you saw yesterday
Tomorrow you will repeat it all again
Then you'll pass blame
But I'll remind you

Ignorance foretells death
You called remember?
Well, here I am
Life and death
One in the same
Take your pick
What does it matter anyway?

I had thrown so many kernels of my corn at the feet of the cat that refused to eat them that I was beginning to think my corn had no value; until a chicken walked by and gave me revelation.

One Bottle, One Glass and Fading Memories

Turn around
I miss the look of your eyes
    and tightly curled red strands hiding portions of your smile
Say the words the way you used to, "darling, I love you"
Then kiss me like you never did
    reading the secrets hidden in my lips
    until you know the thoughts of the heart enamored
    with the soul fading from view

Put the bag down
Please don't take what's left of what love started
Give tomorrow's sun the chance to chase these lingering clouds,
    but if the rain comes, give it the chance to make us clean again

What has been said has been done
Now destined souls seek separation
This damn illusion
Is this what becomes of star-studded skies,
    restless winds
        and the inception of love?
One bottle, one glass and fading memories?

C. L. Brown was born and raised on the island of Jamaica before migrating to the US at 11 years of age. He obtained a Bachelor's Degree in Computer Science from Florida International University and a Master's Degree in Management Information Systems from Nova Southeastern University. One summer's day in the year 2007, a poem called his name. When he answered, it asked him to be its scribe. The result was the first poem he'd ever written, "Love Letter to My Love".

Loud Whispers of Silent Souls is a beautiful collection of poems and inspiring quotes that speak truly of the collective thoughts and experiences of us, the silent souls. You will smile. You will cry. You will love. You will be inspired. You will relate.

For more information, visit www.authorclbrown.com